TOXIC FAITH–
LIBERAL CURE

Bill,

    I wrote chapters 2, 3, 4, and 5. Dave wrote chapter 6.

    You may not always agree, but I hope it provokes serious thinking.

Peace,

Tom & Dave

Toxic Faith– Liberal Cure

Dr. Daniel C. Bruch &
Dr. Thomas W. Strieter

To order additional copies of this book, contact:
Xlibris Corporation
1-888-795-4274
www.Xlibris.com
Orders@Xlibris.com
34446

CONTENTS

THE PREFACE

Who we are

We are two pastors with a combined experience base of about ninety years. Our highest salaries never reached six figures, often even when they were combined. We are liberals. We are liberal pastors. We have given most of our lives in service to others. We have been enmeshed in births and deaths, marriages and divorces, brokenness and restoration, hope and despair, joy and sorrow. We continue to share the real lives of real people. The real people we know are seldom certain about anything, rarely become involved in the public square, but live lives graced with all of the complexities of the human condition. We honor those people, who we believe constitute the great majority of Americans, and are honored and privileged to serve them. We have learned more from them than we have shared and gained more than we have given.

It is the too numerous screamers and shouters of these days that finally edged us into public conversation. We hear them far too often. "Liberals are tax crazy!" No, we are not. "Liberals are baby killers!" No, we are not. "Liberals have a homosexual agenda!" No, we do not. "Liberals are unpatriotic!" No, we are not. "Liberals are against the Bible!" No, we are not. "Liberals want to remove God from the schools!" No, we do not. "Liberals are traitors!" No, we are not. Phrases like these are often loudly shouted by the religious, political, and media segments of the right-wing and they have become catch phrases which have given liberalism a bad name. We remember when "communist!" was shouted at everyone with whom the McCarthyites disagreed. The same kind of name calling is now leveled at liberals. That is dishonest. It is an attempt to define liberals as the cause for many of the things that people fear. This approach has torn the fabric of American society and has transformed healthy diversity into divisive disaster.

What we believe

We believe in justice, freedom, peace, compassion, mercy, responsibility, tolerance, equality, respect, the rule of law, and care for all things. We believe that we are all called to love the poor, the powerless, the disenfranchised, the sick, the imprisoned, the needy, the suffering, and the outsider, because God loves and cares for all people. We believe that we are called to live in love-motivated relationships with all of our world neighbors. We believe that human differences are gifts to be celebrated, not barriers to human relationships. These characteristics, we hold, are exactly what the prophets in the Hebrew Scriptures and Jesus in the Gospels called people of faith to be and to do. Holding to these beliefs does not make us enemies within our society or enemies of our society. Holding to these beliefs cannot be the basis for being attacked with the charge of immorality. No. We believe that there is now a critical necessity for a calm and reasoned response to such assertions so that people of good will, liberal and conservative alike, within all of our political parties, can clarify in their minds what is false and true and where they stand on the issues which have sadly divided our country.

FOREWARD

Purpose, Intent, Focus, and Lens

The purpose of the book

This book has two purposes. The first purpose is to answer those who claim that liberalism is immoral and is somehow destroying the values of this country. Building on that claim, the same people often accuse liberals, on a personal level, of also being immoral and undermining the values of our country. The second purpose is to carefully and rationally deal with many of the most vocalized and divisive current issues in a specifically Judeo-Christian liberal context. We recognize that there are other valid perspectives through which to address these issues and we applaud them. We also hope that our readers include many that come from traditions other than the Judeo-Christian belief system. But we believe that it is a perversion of the Judeo-Christian belief system that has been commandeered by the right. We also think that we liberals have not been very good at having ready and informed responses to the high decibel assertions of the right. We hope that our reasoned and reasonable approach to the essence of the Judeo-Christian belief system will provide courage and support to our compatriots in our mission to restore civility and balance to the conversation.

The intent of the book

It is our intent, therefore, to use quiet and confident scholarship and reason to gently but certainly restore and energize a more informed Judeo-Christian faith. We are speaking of a faith that may hopefully also impact the faithful on the right. We recognize the magnitude of this task. We approach it because of those who, in the name of Jesus and the Judeo-Christian Scriptures, are forcing on the public a distorted and false type of conservatism. It is a radically reactionary and often frightening perspective cloaked in religious language that can ultimately destroy the democratic principles on which our nation is founded. In this book we are calling this segment of the population the fundamentalistic conservatives.

The focus of the book

We are living in a time where "moral values" receive much play in the popular press. Rarely, if ever, however, do the discussions about "moral values" (meaning primarily Judeo-Christian values in our culture) include any serious discussion of what the Jewish and Christian Scriptures actually say about the primary conflicted issues of this day. It is even rarer to come across any attempts to address the question of whether or not Judeo-Christian values may or may not be analogous to liberal values. A moral value has a non-technical definition as follows: a principle, standard, or quality related to the goodness or badness of human action and character. A Judeo-Christian moral value may then be defined as a principle, standard, or quality related to the goodness or badness of human action and character based upon the content of the Judeo-Christian Scriptures. In other words, Judeo-Christian values (those matters and things that are defined as right or wrong, good or evil) are understood to be derived from God, not from reason alone, nor from the human heart, the state, or through majority rule. Seeking to understand if or how Judeo-Christian moral values may be related to liberal values within the context of selected social issues will be that part of our culture upon which we will focus.

The "lens" through which we focus

It is important to remember and understand that all liberals would not endorse everything that is stated here. We have adopted the perspective of the twentieth century American social thinker, Reinhold Niebuhr, as the "lens" through which we focus on social issues. In his classic *Moral Man and Immoral Society*, as well as in his other books, he identified and defined what he called "Christian Realism." Niebuhr was biblically informed, but he fully realized that one cannot take the Christian conception of *agape*, the selfless love of God which we know in Jesus, and demand that a pluralistic, diverse, and often secular society must operate with that ideal. He recognized that such selfless love could not be fully realized this side of the coming kingdom of God. Niebuhr equally realized that we cannot take biblical, particularly Old Testament, laws and demand that secular society be bound by them. Thoughtful Americans realize that this is basic to the concept of separation of church and state. Government is to operate with principles of enlightened reason which promote equal justice under law. The sphere of religion, on the other hand, prophetically (speaking forth) calls government to be faithful to this task, but does not demand that the government operate with specifically Judeo-Christian or biblical principles. As the 16th century reformer, Martin Luther, said, "You can't rule the world with a rosary."

That being the case, Niebuhr said we are to be Christian realists. Societal laws must conform to what he called "rough justice." This kind of justice he calls "rough" because it involves compromise between opposing views. This compromise, however, always strives for equal justice under law, and thus demands moral decision making. Because of the nature of moral compromising, ethically ambiguous decisions are sometimes necessary. Moral decisions in a complex and diverse society are never black/white issues, but always end up in varying shades of gray. Therefore, we as Christians are certainly informed by our faith in the public arena, but the common language of a secular, pluralistic society is the language of informed reason and justice, tempered with mercy. We readily admit that this is a far cry from those elements within the Judeo-Christian community that want to turn government into a theocracy—a rule dominated by religious precepts. The founding fathers wisely refused this approach. Religion can operate freely in American society, but it is not to be entrenched in the decision-making process of working for equal justice under law. In the moment that we would advance a specifically Judeo-Christian agenda, we are infringing on the rights of those who hold different, or no, religious positions.

Liberal and Christian values: a blend

Throughout the pages of this book, we think you will experience a blending of commonly held liberal values as well as Christian values. It will become evident that one of the current and pervasive cultural myths is, indeed, mythological. The myth perpetuated in much of the media, especially on the right, is that God is on the side of conservatives (and the Republican Party) and liberals (and the Democratic Party) are the handmaidens of Satan. While in some specific cases there may be or have been some partial truth to the contention, in general Judeo-Christian values have always been an important part of any liberal political philosophy.

More specifically, if any political orientation can be said to lean in the direction of the teachings of the Christ, it surely seems as though the political left is more oriented in that direction. Issues of poverty and homelessness and health care and strong families and equal justice under the law and caring for the powerless and wounded—all of these concerns and more are currently and traditionally the priority of the political left. This judgment is made for a variety of reasons, including the perception that liberals generally are much more inclusive and accepting of differences, more interested in the needs of others, and feel an obligation to help those who have not yet enjoyed or participated in the common good. Conversely, the current "brand" of conservative fundamentalists seems to insist that they alone are moral while the political left is immoral. In short, moral values are important on some level to all Americans, not just the political right. It harms us all when the term "liberal" is used in a manner that suggests that all liberals are immoral or un-Christian or inferior or any other pejorative adjective. Liberals, Christian or non-Christian, Republican or Democrat, have a demonstrably long history of decision-making based on moral values that are decidedly analogous to Judeo-Christian values. The question is, what do liberals and conservatives have in common in terms of moral values that draw us together toward accomplishing the common good for all?

It is our view that most people have elements of traditional conservatism and liberalism woven within their personal and world views. It is also our view that most of the people to whom we speak and with whom we have regular contact are neither totally "red" nor totally "blue" in the sense of current political jargon. Rather, we see them in varying shades of purple. This includes the fundamentalistic conservatives too. We also share some common values that speak to us about the conflicted issues of the day. What we are not very good at is simply speaking to one another to find those common values that can draw us together.

Our title and perhaps even some of our chapter headings may be seen as somewhat confrontational and edgy with the hope that you may be drawn to the substance of this book. It is the substance that we most want to convey. The title, nonetheless, does convey our perspective on the influence of religious fundamentalistic conservatism on the American scene. For something to be toxic, it must be poisoning the environment. It must be inflicting a harmful ingredient into an otherwise generally healthy organism. While we wish it were not so, the pages that follow seem to give evidence of that reality.

The general and unifying structure of the book

With authorship shared, differences in style and format may occasionally become noticeable. Nonetheless, within such differences we have attempted to include the following structural elements at some place in each chapter: an overview, a historical perspective on the particular issue, claims by fundamentalistic conservatives about the issue, a review of the Judeo-Christian perspective on the issue, a summary and clarification of the liberal perspective, a section on "making a difference," and some final talking points.

1

Saved, Baptized, and Registered! Introducing the Context

Barry Goldwater. 1964. An embarrassing defeat for the Republican Party. Was the base too narrow, made up primarily of the wealthy and the segregationists of the south? Probably so. The solution developed by a group of strategists, calling themselves the New Right, was to expand the base. A young Paul Weyrich founded the Heritage Foundation and the American Legislative Exchange Council to aid in this task. Conservative corporations, foundations, and industries provided easy funding as the ALEC focused on abortion, stopping the ERA, and providing prewritten bills for state legislatures. In 1979 Weyrich coined the term "Moral Majority" and Jerry Falwell became president and provided us with the idea for the chapter heading above. But more of the beginning of the story is below. It pulls together often disparate threads, setting the stage for better understanding the chapters that follow.

Conservative and liberal role playing

We assume conservatives and liberals each have their roles to play. We do recognize and affirm that conservatives (those generally predisposed to resist change) have an important place in society. Humans, cross-culturally, seem to be predominantly resistant to change and most comfortable with the status-quo. It is our judgment that conservatives are not now, never have been, nor ever will be an endangered species. In fact, the difficulty with getting any social movement accomplished is that most people do not want to be moved!

So we confess to you that this comfort with the status-quo is not inherently bad. Without it, sociologists tell us that there would be insufficient social organization for an orderly society. Without a majority of people wanting to stay put where they are and keep working as they are, the consequent social change would likely lead to more social disorganization than a society could long endure. In short, we need conservatives and appreciate the social stability they bring to our culture.

But we also need liberals (those generally predisposed to encourage and support change) to balance, to challenge, and to inspire those who are comfortable with things as they are. Liberals almost always constitute a minority for the reason mentioned above. Liberals constitute a continuing "endangered species" because their disposition toward change confounds the majority, frightens some, worries many, and often challenges predominant societal assumptions. It may be easier not to have us around, but without our balance and impetus toward change, social life would stagnate.

Being right, righteous, and running

The last few decades have brought significant religious change to our culture. Part of that change involves a subgroup of conservatives that has invaded and infected two great American arenas—religion and politics. This subgroup of *fundamentalistic conservatives* (characterized by rigid adherence to selected principles, by intolerance of other views, and by opposition to secularism) came into substantial power with the election of Ronald Reagan. Most are Christians, but some are not. Often they are called the "religious right." We use the term *fundamentalistic* in its dictionary meaning of "hypocritically and excessively" fundamental. They were and still are mostly led by a relatively small group of preachers and political strategists (and a few other self-appointed religious "experts") who are working together to secure control of all facets of American life. The primary vehicle by which they are seizing power across a broad spectrum of American life is religion. It is religion that is a primary and protected social institution, within which we learn our foundational values and beliefs. Religion, as a social institution, and its related values have now been exploited for three decades. Whether those values relate to us personally or in the form of our civil religion (loving our country), these fundamentalistic conservatives have woven together the flag and the cross in a form of unholy commingling that has broken and segmented the heart of America.

The historical roots—In the first half of the twentieth century, much of our country was fully but gently engaged in the struggle between the fundamentals of the Judeo-Christian faith and the enemy called modernism. While many fundamentalists would trace their roots back to the Christian New Testament, the brand of American fundamentalism about which we are speaking can be traced back to the 19th century. If you grew up in a Republican family you were sensitized to issues of morality. If you grew up in a Democratic family, you were sensitized to issues of justice. Republican families were steeped in an ideal culture of hard work, going to church, and personal character. Democratic families were socialized to prioritize the values of diversity and the equitable sharing of the earth's resources. While these were not absolute in character, and likely there was a good bit of blending in families on these issues, these predominant perspectives set the stage for today's happenings. It is the "protestant ethic" (being punctual, hard working, deferring gratification, and prioritizing work) defined by Max Weber (*The Protestant Ethic and the Spirit of Capitalism*, Allen and Unwin: Cornwall, 1930) that characterized the Republicans of the time and, in fact, identified the predominant norm in the culture for at least a century.

In that same general timeframe, the cultural impact of a series of twelve tracts written between 1910 and 1915 and titled *The*

Fundamentals was well established. These fundamentals included the belief that the Bible was without error, that the world was created in six 24 hour days, that the Bible was accurate in matters of science and history, that Jesus was divine and of virgin birth, that Jesus died on a cross to redeem humankind and would return to judge at the second coming. Some also believed that the King James Version of the Judeo-Christian Scriptures was the only correct translation.

Also at the same time that *The Fundamentals* were written and published, the same people that adhered to these beliefs were beginning to feel displaced by the recurring waves of southern and eastern European immigrants. These immigrants were predominantly not Protestants and became the impetus for the predominantly northern European whites (sometimes called the "old stock whites") to feel betrayed by their leaders. They felt that our leaders had led our nation into a war with Germany that never was adequately resolved but did introduce us (an unintended consequence) to the "evils" of biblical criticism which began in Germany. Biblical criticism is the examination of the literary origins and historical values of the books composing the Bible. This feeling of betrayal quickly led to criticism of the teaching of evolution in our schools and the perceived elitism of professionalized educators who, in their minds, seemed to scorn traditional family values.

So it was already in the 1920's that battles were being pursued through the courts, the state legislatures, and their various denominations. The now famous "Monkey Trial" took place during this time (1925) in Dayton, Tennessee. The fundamentalist, William Jennings Bryon, was opposed by the atheist, Clarence Darrow. The results were mixed and the effects linger to this day. It was here also that the first of many general conventions of mainline Protestant denominations found themselves in conflict between the fundamentalists and the modernists.

This type of fundamentalistic conservatism continued to grow in the 1930's with the establishment of parochial schools, colleges, seminaries, and missionary societies. They also moved into areas of media to share their beliefs and concerns, especially into the print and radio media. During this time the rise of parachurch organizations began, seeking to meet the needs of specific cohorts of people. They were also deeply committed to passing this system of beliefs on to their children. So what began before World War I, grew thereafter to produce huge pentecostal, charismatic, and evangelical movements after World War II, and set the stage for the fundamentalistic conservatives of our day.

Contemporary realities—A look at the more immediate past finds the fundamentalists greatly affected by the massive cultural changes of the 1960's: the women's liberation movement, the sexual revolution, the youth movement colloquially called the "hippies," the civil rights movement, the Vietnam anti-war movement, and the rise of numerous alternative religions (Moonies, Hari Krishna, etc,). Many people were not supportive of such dramatic cultural shifts.

At the same time, these notorious changes were matched by Supreme Court decisions that seemed to add authenticity and cultural approval to many of them. Some of these included banning official prayer and Bible reading in public schools (Engel v. Vitale, 1962), the right to counsel for all (Gideon v. Wainright, 1963), the right to know your rights (Miranda v. Arizona, 1966), a clarification of free speech (Tinker v. Des Moines, 1969), limits on government involvement in private schools (Lemon v. Kurtzman, 1971), legalized abortion in the first trimester (Roe v. Wade, 1973), and limits on the confidentiality of presidential communication (USA v. Nixon, 1974).

As could be expected, the subgroup of fundamental conservatives, the fundamentalistic conservatives, quickly responded with an untested and fairly unknown cast of characters that have since become household words—Jimmy Swaggart, Jim Bakker, Oral Roberts, Pat Robertson, Jerry Falwell, and Phyllis Shlafly, to name a few. While diverse in background and skill, they were unified in their defense of the traditional Judeo-Christian values. They were skilled at defining these values within the context of a simpler time set in rural and small town America. These values—Biblical authority in all areas of life, faith in Jesus Christ, a lifestyle based on Biblical values—were shared in a manner that granted them broad appeal beyond just the fundamentalistic conservatives. So wide was the appeal that George Gallop declared 1976 as "the year of the evangelical." Even national news magazines ran cover stories about the rapid rise of evangelical Protestantism. The mainline churches, on the other hand, seemed confused and demoralized by this phenomenon as the ranks of their own members were shrinking.

The present—Today we are living with the results of thirty years of increasing success on the part of the fundamentalistic conservatives. We are being subjected to a massive and continuing religious, political, and social assault on another set of long-held and highly esteemed values. These values are embodied in our Constitution and extol the virtues mentioned in the Introduction—tolerance, justice and the rule of law, human rights, diversity, equality, freedom, social responsibility, protection of the environment, strong families. In an attempt to return to some unidentifiable past, we are subjected in unprecedented multi-media blitzes to "return God to our schools," to "return Christian values to the Supreme Court," to "restore government to the Christian values of our founders," and the like. For example, recently the School Board in Dover, PA instituted a new policy requiring all ninth-grade biology teachers to read a statement on "Intelligent Design" before teaching evolution lessons. The district is believed to be the first in the country to require such a disclaimer. Shortly thereafter, however, a judge ruled the policy to be illegal. Studies, in fact, do show that American children are falling behind children in other nations in their knowledge and understanding of science. However, allowing science education to be watered down by zealots who seek to use our public schools as pulpits from which to teach ideology as fact, while denying teachers and students their basic right to religious freedom, will not help the matter. Religion undeniably has its place in American society, but that place is not our public schools!

Throughout this assault on our values, a primary Judeo-Christian value seems to have been lost—the ends never justify the means. We acknowledge that there are some who question the absoluteness of that value, citing situations where the importance of the ends might require questionable means. We leave it to others to continue that debate. We would remind those who question that value, however, that if one takes even the slightest step toward questionable means in order to achieve some exemplary end, then where does one draw the line thereafter? In the case of our current federal administration, it appears that any means seem to be justified in search of the end—a theocracy where those in power determine what their god wants so that they might impose it on the rest of us. There can be seen no apparent acknowledgement that the Founder of the Christian faith taught and lived in a manner that decried power (the ability to coerce even against one's will) and replaced it with service—to God and to one another.

Concurrent with the rise of fundamentalistic conservatism came a very sad reality. The mood of our country began to turn mean spirited. Our public discourse and our private social intercourse became increasingly hostile as individual anger rose. Part of this anger was and still is related to many of those changes in the world around us, and mentioned above, that challenge our security, stability, and comfort. This is an expected part of such change. But what we are speaking of here is not the normal change inherent within our society but the orchestrated and professionally engineered anger that has become a part of both our public and private conversations. You can crisscross this country and see the same slogans shared in the same tone about the same issues that have come to provide the power base for these fundamentalistic conservatives. You can ask almost anyone on the streets and in similar language and with similar anger hear the ranting and railing about some of our elected leaders that seems very much out of proportion to the reality at hand. It is within this context that the word "liberal" has come to embody all that is wrong with our country and most of the social institutions around which our common needs are addressed.

Most of this has been accomplished by using communication strategies, and particularly propaganda devices, that distort, manipulate, mislead, deceive, and even coerce our fellow citizens.

They have used images, myths, symbols, fears, and statements to gain social and political control. They have moved beyond fundamentalism as a type or mode of religious belief to a system of mass manipulation and political power, with an avowed aspiration to attain dominant control. And they have been very good at it.

Perhaps using propaganda devices as the primary example of how this can be and has been accomplished would be helpful. In the fairly recent past, most secondary and college level students learned about propaganda and how it can be used to subvert the truth. In most of the current textbooks that we examined, any topics related to the use of propaganda rarely if ever appeared. Yet, the necessity for an informed and critically thinking public is an essential that our founding fathers championed. To help what seems to be a knowledge deficit, here are the most obvious and most used propaganda devices with examples of how the fundamentalistic conservatives have used them:

Name Calling—Without concern for the truth, this type of propaganda appeals to our fears, prejudices, and hatreds. Bad names or bad labels are given to individuals, nations, races, groups of people, ideas, or beliefs that the propagandist wants to condemn. For example, when Sean Hannity in his book *Deliver Us From Evil* said, "Liberals are more tolerant of Saddam Hussein than they are of George W. Bush," he was name calling by suggesting that all liberals preferred Saddam Hussein over George W. Bush.

Association—Here the propagandist attempts to establish a relationship between a person or idea and someone or something or an object or cause that people respect. Often the flag or church or Uncle Sam or an important person are used. For example, when George W. Bush once said that "I believe that God wants me to be president," he was associating himself in a positive way with God.

Glittering Generalities—This is when propagandists identify themselves or their programs with highly loaded "virtue" words, usually appealing to love, loyalty, brotherhood/sisterhood, patriotism, honor, truth, freedom, etc. The desire is to get us to simply accept something without examining the evidence. An example would be when we are told that "It is the patriotic duty of this Christian nation to fight for democracy and freedom."

The Bandwagon Technique—This is the "everybody's doing it" approach. It's purpose is to convince us to follow the crowd and accept something as a whole without examining the evidence. For example, the t-shirt that says, "Pro-Choice Christians? There Aint' None!" In other words, make sure you are on the bandwagon of "pro-lifers."

Testimonials—This technique is when a respected or hated person is used to say that a given idea or group or program or person is good or bad.

Repeating a Lie—We have all heard the old adage that if you repeat a lie often enough, people will soon believe it. All one needs to do these days is check numerous sources on the web to find daily summaries of lies told by numerous people, including George W. Bush (www.bushwatch.com).

The "Plain Folks" Technique—This is when the propagandist tries to convince people that her/his ideas are good because they represent everyday common people. This is the technique George W. Bush used when he said that "they want the President, in this modern era, to be something they can relate to. Someone who they don't think is intellectually intimidating. Someone who isn't really lost in the big fog of intellectual ideas and the world of words." In other words, he is saying that he is just a common person.

Card Stacking—This is selecting only those facts, real or imagined, that support the propagandists point of view. The daily White House press briefing is an example of this, as are most editorials.

Slanted Words—This technique is when one's choice of words gives an imprecise or false meaning. For example, when Bill Clinton said that he "did not have sexual relations with that woman," it turned out he clearly did have a sexual relationship with that woman. He tried to play games with the definition of "sexual relations" and it just got him into deeper trouble.

False Syllogisms—A syllogism is made up of two premises from which a conclusion can be drawn. In a false syllogism, the conclusion drawn from the first two statements is wrong. For example, (1) All liberals believe taxes should be shared equitably, (2) Karl Rove believes taxes should be shared equitably, (3) therefore Karl Rove is a liberal.

Viewing the world from its endpoint

What broad world view do fundamentalistic conservatives share? While most devout Christians throughout this planet seek to "live in the world, but not of the world," this brand of fundamentalists passionately pursues and embraces the material world with its technology and marketing strategies to support their manipulation. They reject good works as a part of a rejection of the "social gospel," but esteem and highly exalt the economic and political gospels of republicanism, nationalism, and free-market capitalism. They seem to be much less concerned about the gospel of salvation for humankind and more concerned about using religion as a weapon in the ideological conquest of our country. They do not seem interested in influencing opinions and beliefs using reason and civil argument but rather seek the power to insist on their own opinions and beliefs through the tools of church and state. They seem experts at the propaganda device of telling a lie often enough until it becomes the "truth." They just keep moving on knowing that they will soon be into another news story and the press will move on too and the public will forget the distortion and lies just perpetrated. They have learned well the tactics of the grade school playground bullies— whoever shouts the loudest and the longest wins. They seem to know that subtle and not so subtle forms of slander, bullying, intimidation, fear, and all sorts of dirty tricks will work.

To be more specific . . . .—Numerous recent books have already been written about how fundamentalistic conservatives view the world. The following is a brief summary of some of the basic concepts that provide the framework for their perspective on the world—a framework that helps to provide the energy, the goals, and the processes as they pursue the ideological conquest of America as mentioned just above.

1) The Second Coming, or the End Times, predominates much of their thinking. Essentially, they believe that the Bible details an accurate timeline leading to the end of the world as we know it. Followers of several varieties of current apocalyptic thinking (dispensationalists, reconstructionists, dominionists) link that timeline to such diverse things as 9/11, gay marriages, climate changes, and increased natural disasters. While details vary among its adherents, primary among their world view is the belief that Christ will only initiate his second coming when the world has prepared a proper place for him. For them, the first step is in Christianizing the USA. To accomplish this, some of the Biblical prophesies are translated into political action.

   For the dominionists, this Christian domination would bring an end to the separation of church and state, the removal of all government social programs and replacing them with Christian church programs, and replacing our democracy with a theocracy ruled by Old Testament law. For the reconstructionists, one could add the removal of all government regulatory agencies because they distract from the goal of Christianizing America. The goal is to conquer America for Christianity so that Jesus can finally return.

2) Another perspective of the fundamentalistic conservatives is that which originated in the Project for a New American Century (PNAC) in 1997. It is based on the example of Pax Romana (27 BC-180 AD) which is Latin for "the Roman peace." Pax Romana was a period of relative peace experienced by states within the Roman Empire. The term stems most correctly from the reality that Roman rule and its legal system pacified regions, sometimes forcefully, which had suffered from war among rivals. It was not a peaceful era because rebellions were frequent. Nonetheless, most mischief was stopped and one could live also in peace as long as the Roman Empire was not challenged.

With this historical precedent, the PNAC developed policies designed to create "a new world order" which they labeled Pax Americana, or "the American peace." Some of the most notable signatories were Richard Cheney, Jeb Bush, Paul Wolfowitz, and Donald Rumsfeld. This concept became official policy in late 2002 when the Bush administration's first National Security Strategy was released. This 31 page document asserted American dominance as the lone superpower. It acknowledged and affirmed this status that no rival power would be allowed to challenge. It also said that the reason the world should accept this state of affairs is because it would provide for the expansion of peace and more freedom. A Pax Americana would be "in the service of a balance of power that favors freedom."

At the time it was announced, critics described the new strategy as arrogant and dangerous, especially given the tone of humility in foreign affairs that President Bush promised in his inaugural address. To supporters, however, including the present-day fundamentalistic conservatives, it represented an overdue codification of America's mission of global leadership. It provided a reason for "pre-emptive" war if that war would enhance freedom in the world. And, similar to all previous attempts at empire-building (Persian, Babylonian, Roman, Ottoman, Spanish, or British), they exploited religion to give their empire dreams divine legitimacy in the eyes of their true believers.

3) A third building block of fundamentalistic conservatives is the belief that our society is involved in a cultural war. The cornerstone of this war is a major offensive against Christianity. They believe that the popular media constantly delivers this message. Further, they believe that such "intolerant and divisive views" that now prevail in our culture are initiated by and held by America's self-professed intellectual elite and, especially, the left-wing radicals who control the Democrat Party. They surely also believe that these views are held by a strong majority of the mainstream media. (A recent Pew Research Center for People and

Policy poll conducted in May 2005 shows just the opposite—
the media are conservative while the majority of Americans
hold liberal attitudes on most social issues.)

They hold, correctly, that religious principles are
fundamentally a part of our heritage. They wonder, then,
why they are under such violent attack. Summarizing, they
suggest two reasons. The first is that they are convinced
that the goal of all liberals is to bring about a governmental
system of state socialism. Liberals, in their opinion, believe
that the state is to provide for the satisfaction of human
needs instead of God and the individual. In fact, they believe
that socialism requires that citizens show reverence and
deference to the state as the god-like source from which all
blessings flow. The supreme State can have no other god
before it. A second reason is that they see what they define
as lobbying interests and special interests seeking laws that
make certain sins out to be virtues. These liberals seek the
validation of the law, in the futile belief that the legal right
to be wrong makes wrong right.

Finally, they define much of our judiciary as arrogant,
with judges defining as bigotry those matters that they
define as moral discernment. These same judges tell them
that the Constitution does not grant them the right to
establish the rules of civility and set the standards of decency
by which they wish to live. In short, they believe that the
Constitution no longer protects them but has become, in
the hands of unaccountable, power-corrupted judges, an
instrument of their oppression.

4)   The fourth area really blends a number of working concepts
that provide understanding and meaning to the
fundamentalistic conservatives. A primary concept is the
understanding that the Western Judeo-Christian traditions
have worked well for several centuries, so why change or
revise them now? It is in changing the predominant cultural
values and legitimizing alternatives that concerns are raised.
A second concept is that for the fundamentalistic
conservatives, it is not easy to differentiate between public

and private areas of life. For example, it would be very difficult for them to support Roe v. Wade while holding a contrary private view. Third, they believe in certain moral absolutes that are as unchangeable to them as mathematical absolutes. These absolutes are value-based (the sanctity of an unborn life, for example) and so they assume everyone can clearly see them and should hold them too. Fourth, they believe that the proper role of government is to promote moral excellence, righteousness, and goodness. They do not believe that government's role is to interfere in the workplace or marketplace.

Based on these elements of their world view, and by various means, these fundamentalistic conservatives have become an intrusion in all of our lives. One of the substantial historic changes their leaders have inflicted on us is that they have not limited their interests to religion. They have not stayed within the framework of our historical church-state relationships, but have fully engaged religious participation in politics. While lawyers and courts will continue to debate and decide on the meaning of the establishment clause ("Congress shall make no law respecting an establishment of religion . . . .") of the First Amendment, the reality remains that the activities of this subgroup of fundamentalists have moved from the domain of private belief into the very open sphere of the public arena. They have made their brand of religion a very urgent public business. And again, the "demon" in all of this was variously defined as "modernism" (accommodation to cultural change) and "liberalism" (eagerness to engage change), and these designations were continually used to develop division and conflict between peoples. In reality, this process became the means whereby political and social debates and disputes were redefined in religious terms.

So here we are—We now find the public debate formulated by fundamentalistic religious ideologies. This debate is often framed by supposed biblical arguments, using literalistic rhetoric and code words, couched in emotional terms, and mixed together with a new brew of patriotic, religious, and free-market zealotry. Not only that. What once began as a seemingly innocent exercise of tax breaks and other perks accorded non-profit and religious institutions, became the vehicle whereby they became media moguls. Mixing with those in the secular world that had been "converted," they have now blended into private and public media power brokers who possess virtually every available means to enter into the privacy of our family rooms, our minds, and into our daily lives disseminating information with ulterior political and religious ends.

So if we now limit our definition of fundamentalistic conservatism to those who currently hold political power in our country, we would say that they are defined as opposing big government, abortion, gun control, environmentalism, affirmative action (a form of civil rights) and homosexuality. They do not, however, oppose everything; they are also defined as supporting religion in politics, school prayer, creationism (the current jargon term is "intelligent design") and the military (at least with regard to spending, not necessarily serving).

If we define them by their actions, the definitions become much less clear. The most outspoken and angry among those who seemed to hate President Clinton have had their own sexual lapses; the most righteous of the publicly righteous have also been tripped up by numerous common sins. They seem to have abandoned fiscal responsibility, having broken even President Reagan's record budget deficits. They are living one of the most remarkable position changes in our time, perhaps as important as the South's going Republican in the 1970s. They have been responsible through fiscal hemorrhaging to see the liberals replacing conservatives as the champions of fiscal responsibility. They have also abandoned smaller government by continuing to add to the federal payroll. According to Stephen Slivinski, director of budget studies at the Cato Institute (a conservative think tank), "President Bush has presided over the largest overall increase in inflation-adjusted federal spending since Lyndon B. Johnson. Even after excluding spending on defense and homeland security,

Bush is still the biggest-spending president in 30 years. His 2006 budget doesn't cut enough spending to change his place in history, either." In addition, "Total Government spending grew by 33 percent during Bush's first term. The federal budget as a share of the economy grew from 18.5 percent of GDP on Clinton's last day in office to 20.3 percent by the end of Bush's first term." As for the activities of the Republican controlled Congress, they have "enthusiastically assisted the budget bloat. Inflation-adjusted spending on the combined budgets of the 101 largest programs they vowed to eliminate in 1995 has grown by 27 percent. The GOP was once effective at controlling nondefense spending. The final nondefense budgets under Clinton were a combined $57billion smaller than what he proposed from 1996 to 2001.Under Bush, Congress passed budgets that spent a total of $91 billion more than the president requested for domestic programs. Bush signed every one of those bills during his first term. Even if Congress passes Bush's new budget exactly as proposed, not a single cabinet-level agency will be smaller than when Bush assumed office."

As for accountability, the blame always seems to lie elsewhere. They are bipartisan only when others agree with them. The only social security they seem interested in is that which would accrue to financial brokers should "privatization" of Social Security become a reality. In terms of peace, they appear to think that it is best attained by pre-emptive war and that staying the course means an unquestioned adherence to failed policies regardless of how bad the situation has become.

So, as the bumper sticker asks, what exactly are the conservatives conserving? For the current fundamentalistic conservatives, economic conservatism is gone, and social conservatism is under unexpected attack by some of their own. What's left that binds this fundamental brother/sisterhood together? What holds them unified in spite of violating most of the dearly held principles of conservatism? Robbed finally even of conservative doctrine, these fundamentalistic conservatives have a unique glue to bind them together. It is the thing that stands out in every setting, separates them from others, and remains after all those traditional values have fallen away. It is their anger. It is anger at a world that doesn't fit their ideas about how the world ought to be. It is a world that continues to change in spite of their intimidation and shouting in the halls of Congress and over the many talk shows that give energy to it. It is an anger that is in the process of destroying the very power they have come to love, to use, and to abuse.

Viewing the future with hope

So what might it be that can finally get liberals and conservatives speaking to one another again? We know that most of us share many of the same values, principles, and beliefs that could draw us together. We know that it is un-Christian to close down the possibility of discovering practical and authentic truth in those with whom we disagree. Affirming this point brings both justice and charity and acknowledges that it is essential for any kind of inquiry. It is also a matter of good judgment and enlightened self-interest to be open to the possibility of discovering additional or different truth in this manner. Finally, we commit ourselves to the understanding that there is risk in seeking to enter into the heart and mind of the person with whom one is conversing. Without taking that risk, however, we cannot work in the direction of a common good.

Our primary concern, then, continues to be the promotion and extension of civilized conversation among liberals and with conservatives. The phrase *civilized conversation* may seem rather cold and clinical, but it represents an essential means of human relating. When conversation descends to uncivilized behavior, the major priority is given to winning the argument, stilling or subduing the opponent, or simply coming out on top in some manner. Without civilized conversation, it is difficult to be at peace with diverse religious, political, or cultural groups. Without civilized conversation, maintaining peace among nations cannot be accomplished. In addition, uncontrolled biases make conversation impossible because they make listening with an open mind impossible. It is only in the fairly recent past that the phenomenon of uncivilized confrontation has come to appear daily on our television screens. We see it in various iterations of shouting matches, including between groups that are advocating causes that are in conflict. We regularly see it between political, religious, and cultural cohorts. We hope to see it dissipate as we also hope to be a small part of its amelioration.

Making a difference

Here are a few ideas for gaining a better understanding of the events that have brought us to this place in our society and how we might respond as individuals:

- Take the required time and attention to seek understanding about how one might separate information from substantive knowledge and substantive knowledge from ideology.
- Seek to understand and engage the anxieties and ethical dilemmas that science has produced.
- Engage in an active search of neutral information about the influence of secular humanism on our culture and society.
- Work hard to ameliorate sectarian strife that almost always endangers the freedom of everyone.
- The fundamentalistic conservatives have, though their activities, redefined Christians as a political/social movement. They have defined Republican values as the same as Christian values. As such, church and state have become improperly blended. Work to restore the proper relationship of separation between church and state.

Talking points

- **We Assume Conservatives and Liberals Each Have Their Role to Play.** Our society, indeed, we think every society, is best served with a balance between those citizens resistant to change and those citizens predisposed toward change. On the whole, there are generally more people resistant to change than those eager to engage change. It has always been the primary difficulty of social reformers to find followers to engage in change.

- **The Last Few Decades Have Brought Significant Change.** During the last thirty years, a subgroup of fundamentalist conservatives has been working together to acquire control of all aspects of American life. While the roots can be traced to the late 19th century, it was in the early 20th century that their beliefs became more focused. The primary social institution they used and are using to accomplish this social control is religion. The use of propaganda and other communication strategies have been effective tools for them.

- **What Broad World View Do Fundamentalistic Conservatives Share?** The basic concepts that provide understanding to the views of the fundamentalist conservatives include: 1) their belief that Christ will only initiate His second coming when the world has prepared a proper place for Him, namely, the USA when it is Christianized; 2) the belief in a new world order which they labeled Pax Americana, or "the American peace"; 3) the conviction that our society is involved in a cultural war, the cornerstone of which is a major offensive against Christianity; and 4) the assumption that the Western Judeo-Christian traditions have worked well for several centuries, so why change or revise them now?

2

My Country Right or Wrong?

Stephen Decatur, a naval officer during the War of 1812, coined the phrase, "Our country right or wrong." Carl Schurz, a civil war general and senator, said it differently: "Our country, right or wrong; when right to be kept right; when wrong to be set right." These are two patriotic visions. This chapter discusses which of these interpretations best serves the fulfillment of the American vision.

Americans, no matter how their views might otherwise differ, can generally agree that a patriot is a person who has an ardent love for his or her country. Nevertheless, in spite of this common definition, there can be a great divide between conservatives and liberals over the issue of how this patriotic devotion is to be expressed. Let's refer to a recent subject as an example. During the eight years of the Clinton administration, beginning long before the Lewinski debacle, conservatives in some circles were almost brutal in their devastating attacks on President Clinton. Although their criticisms were considered by many as unnecessarily hateful, most Americans nevertheless viewed them as part of the give-and-take of our political discourse. It seems curious, then, that today the patriotic loyalty of anyone who questions the policies of the current administration, particularly related to war and terrorism, is called into question.

Clearly, the whole business of attacking people's patriotism because they hold different views calls for a clarification of what patriotism actually means.

Patriotism or chauvinism?

There is a difference between patriotism and chauvinism. It is our belief that thoughtful patriots understand the complexities involved in our love relationship with our country. Patriotism does not mean, "My country, right or wrong," as Stephen Decatur said in a toast. The fervor of our patriotism and our understanding of what defines patriotism can change as circumstances change. Do we, in a given set of circumstances, stand *with* our governmental policies, or do we take our stand as the loyal opposition? Certainly, it is always *our country*, but that does not mean we are to go along with what is wrong!

As Albert Camus, the noted philosopher, said, "I should be able to love my country and still love justice."

If we listen to some of the strident right-wing talk shows currently dominating the air waves, we don't need to wait very long before we hear liberals being called unpatriotic for their questioning of administration policies or for having differing viewpoints on the war, family values, abortion, or other conflicted issues of the day. The very nature of the American system, however, is that it calls for ongoing debate and differences of opinion in the public arena. To believe otherwise is to operate with a misguided understanding of patriotism.

If liberals are perceived by some as unpatriotic, it is because the very meaning of patriotism has been distorted. Rather than patriotism, *chauvinism* has become the order of the day. The word comes from Nicholas Chauvin, a soldier in Napoleon's army who was blindly loyal to him. Chauvinism is zealous and aggressive patriotism, a conviction that we are better because we are chosen. It expresses itself in excessive enthusiasm for military glory and holds no room for difference of opinion.

We are a government "of, by, and for the people," as Abraham Lincoln said. That means that policies are forged in the public forum as well as in the halls of Congress. To deny differences of opinion and to brand them as unpatriotic is to squelch the very instrument by which democracy lives and breathes. The great tragedy of our time is that open debate is largely lost, and the shrill voices of name calling and condemnation have taken the place of civility and dialogue.

If chauvinism is what patriotism is, then liberals are decidedly unpatriotic! There has been a continuous stream of chauvinism in American history that has equated belligerent patriotism and suspicion toward other nations and people, both foreign and domestic, with true patriotism. This mentality has been divisive in American society. In the 19th century for instance, a nativist group called "know-nothings" because they refused to publicize their basic philosophy, directed their anger toward immigrants, Catholics, and whoever or whatever else wasn't "*like us*." Their purpose was to fight against "foreign influence" in the name of upholding what they perceived as the American view. Among other things, they worked to elect only native-born Americans to office and to place limitations on eligibility for citizenship. Though the "know-nothing" movement died in time, remnants of its spirit are alive and well and living among us as evidenced in the current debates over immigration reform.

This distorted idea of patriotism occurred again after World War II. Obsessed with finding communists under every rock, Senator Joseph McCarthy and the House Un-American Activities Committee, like Don Quixote jousting with windmills, hysterically raised America's temperature to the boiling point by lashing out at perceived enemies of the state. McCarthy charged that communists had infiltrated the State Department, but he offered little or no evidence. The communist witch hunt that ensued ruined many reputations and careers, including numerous Hollywood screen writers. But this crisis in American history, like others before it, finally faded out, and McCarthy ended his days in alcoholic oblivion.

We are living in difficult and fearful times when well-meaning people, looking to their elected leaders for security, are vulnerable to those who prey on their fears. In such times, chauvinistic policies and attitudes can easily gain ascendancy. One can see this happening today. Consider the anti-French sentiment that arose after France refused to support our government's Iraqi war plans, resulting in the serving of "freedom fries" in the congressional cafeteria and the boycotting of French wines. Patriotism, for many, has once again become equated with blind acceptance of government policies. Amid the shouting, wiser and more mature voices have been almost muted, and the noble visions on which America was founded have been distorted, to the detriment of our future viability as a nation. In the words of the book of Proverbs 29:18, "when there is no vision, the people perish." Once again it is time for people and political groups who live by the vision of America's democratic ideals to assert themselves against the destructive policies of the contemporary "know-nothings" and chauvinists. This is essential if we truly love our country and if justice and decency will again prevail.

Well, isn't America a Christian nation?

Before we get further into the discussion of what patriotism properly means in the American democratic scheme of things, it is necessary, first of all, to correct a false impression, held by many fundamentalistic conservatives, that our founding fathers intended for America to be a Christian nation and that we are God's chosen people. In this sense then, to be truly patriotic, one must also be a Christian. We are constantly told by these folks that America's troubles are due to the fact that we have left the Christian moorings which our Christian founding fathers intended for this nation. These religious leaders, and the people they represent, want to return to some mythic past when everyone (at least those involved in the formation of the American republic) was, according to them, Christian. They say that they want a "Christ-centered America," where creationism is taught as science in the public classroom; where prayer, usually in the name of Jesus, is permitted in public schools; where all abortions are eliminated by striking down Roe v Wade; where there is a constitutional ban on same-sex marriage—all these policies, and more, in the name of protecting "family values." (We will argue elsewhere that their understanding of upholding family values often doesn't deal with the real issues.) Such viewpoints reflect the spirit of the Puritan clergyman, Cotton Mather, who believed that America is the nation chosen by God. They do not, however, reflect the spirit of the founding fathers who were fearful of religious interference in the rule of law, and who very deliberately separated church and state.

Cotton Mather (1663-1728) was active during the period known as the "First Great Awakening" (1675-1750) in the American colonies, when, particularly through revivals, there was an upsurge of religious fervor and church participation. Mather wrote a treatise entitled *Magnalia Christi Americana (The Great Acts of Christ in America)*, in which he compared the settlement of New England to Israel leaving Egypt in the Exodus and settling in the Promised Land. This new American experience in New England, Mather said, indicates that the colonists were the new chosen people in the new promised land. This treatise was highly influential for a while, but by the time of the American Revolution, it was quite forgotten. This may be due to the fact that from 1750 to 1800 America was in a state of religious decline.

The "chosen America" idea, however, was revived in what is called the "Second Great Awakening," starting in 1801 when a great religious revival began again. With the expansion westward in the 19th century, Mather's ideas of chosenness and destiny once again became popular, and the concept of "manifest destiny" became the rallying cry that swept throughout the country. "This land is mine," was expressed as the epitome of manifest destiny, and the seizure of the land often was carried out with arrogance of power and aggression. The slaughter of Native Americans and the exploitation of slaves, who served as the engine that propelled much of 19th century economy, are two examples. Even now in the 21st century, this belief that we are God's chosen ones is prevalent especially among religious fundamentalists who insist that therefore it is our destiny as Christians to rule the world. The case can be argued that we are still in that second great awakening and still experiencing the effects of its fundamentalist spirit.

t in calling America a Christian nation
ıristian principles are operating with a
at is being foisted on the American people.
:alled instead for a secular state, where
.... ɩo operate in a voluntary way, and they
insisted on the separation of church and state. The U.S.
Constitution says very clearly that "there shall be no established
religion."

Historians tell us, as we noted earlier, that during the
Revolutionary period between 1750 and 1800, the influence of
the Christian church and its beliefs was at its lowest ebb in the
history of America. In fact, the few Christian ministers who
spoke out between 1787 and 1789 denounced the proposed
Constitution as godless, anti-Christian, Jewish, Islamic, deistic,
pagan, and atheistic. It has been said that at that time in our
history, perhaps as few as between six and eleven percent of
the American people were actively involved in the Christian
church. Surely, some of the founding fathers were Christians.
Many of them, however, were not Christians at least in the
conventional understanding of the word. Certainly this could
be said about the most influential of those who drafted the
Declaration of Independence and the Constitution.

Most of our country's founders were rationalists who operated
with reason alone, and many of them were deists. Rationalists
held that any claim to supernatural revelation was false. John
Adams even felt that organized religion was harmful. Many of
the founders who were deists, including Washington, Adams,
Jefferson and Franklin among many others, believed that the
course of nature gave evidence to the existence of God, but they
felt that formal religion was unnecessary. Thomas Jefferson, in
fact, spent a good deal of time in the presidential office going
through the four Gospels, culling out anything that smacked of
the miraculous or that supported the deity of Jesus. His intent
was to whittle down the Gospels until he came up with the pure
ethical teachings of Jesus. He felt these were of great value, as
long as they were in accord with the principles of reason, justice,
and mercy.

It is even dubious whether George Washington knelt in prayer at Valley Forge. As a deist, Washington did not believe in a personal God who responded to prayer. This story of kneeling in prayer is one of a number of stories manufactured by Parson Weems, who wrote a semi-fictionalized biography of Washington that was published after Washington's death. Such stories, along with the "I cannot tell a lie, I cut down the cherry tree" account, most likely came out of Parson Weems' imagination. But such stories greatly influenced generations of people, particularly the young, during the era of the Second Great Awakening, beginning in 1801. Our intent is not to desecrate the memory of the founding fathers in any way, but to set the story straight about their religious beliefs. We must say it again: The fathers of our constitution were not in the Christian religion business! It was the United States Treaty of Tripoli, Article 11 (negotiated during Washington's administration, then unanimously ratified by the U.S. Senate and signed by President Adams in 1797) that said "[T]he government of the United States of America is not in any sense founded on the Christian Religion." This statement in no way denigrates the role of religion in the formation of American history; however, the record must be made clear: the crucial period in the formation of the American republic—1750 to 1800—was marked by rationalism which is reflected in our founding documents. No latter day revisionism by the religious right will change that fact.

Living up to our ideals

Patriotism holds America to the high ideals on which it was founded. One of the ideals embodied in our country's founding documents is that our government is charged with the responsibility to serve the common good. The founding fathers were greatly influenced by Thomas Paine, who in his pamphlet of 1776, *Common Sense*, fanned the flames in the American colonies, not only for independence from England, but more importantly, for a new democratic ideal. Paine espoused *republicanism*—not a specific form of government, but a "government constituted for '*respublica* . . . or the public good,' as opposed to one that served 'despotic' ends." (See Harvey J. Kaye, *Thomas Paine and the Promise of America,* p. 47, Hill and Wang, N.Y., 2005.) Paine's vision was of a representative democracy. "By ingrafting representation upon democracy," he said, "we arrive at a system of government capable of embracing and confederating all the various interests and every extent of territory and population." (ibid.)

Our founding fathers, sons of the era of rationalism, drafted our country's foundational documents on the principles of reason and equal justice under law. The Declaration of Independence recognizes the importance of striving for the "common good" when it states that "We hold these truths to be self-evident, that *all* (italics are ours) men [people] are created equal, and are endowed by their Creator with certain fundamental, unalienable rights, and among these are life, liberty, and the pursuit of happiness." Similarly, the U.S. Constitution was consciously drafted to reflect these same ideals. Later on in our history, the pledge of allegiance faithfully reflects the spirit of the founding fathers by pledging allegiance to ". . . the republic . . . one nation, indivisible, with liberty and justice for all." Unfortunately, these important words often seem to be forgotten in all the current squabbling over the words "under God," which were added in 1954 during the Eisenhower administration.

There is yet another ideal reflected in our founding documents that is especially germane to our situation today. Consistent with the principles of liberty and justice for all, the founding fathers insisted on the separation of church and state. They had known state-established religions and religious persecution in their past, and they would have no more of it. Thus, the Constitution states that "there shall be no established religion,"—though voluntary religion would operate within the system without impediments. James Madison, a principal author of the Constitution and Bill of Rights and the fourth U.S. president, summarized his views on separation of church and state by noting that ". . . . it may not be easy, in every possible case, to trace the line of separation between the rights of religion and civil authority with such distinctness as to avoid collusions and doubts on unessential points. The tendency of a usurpation on one side or the other, *or to a corrupting coalition or alliance between them* (emphasis ours), will be best guarded by an entire abstinence of the Government from interference in any way whatever, beyond the necessity of preserving public order, and protecting each sect against trespass on its legal rights by others." (Quoted by Robert L. Maddox in *Separation of Church and State: Guarantor of Religious Freedom*, New York: Crossroad, 1987, p. 39.) Nearly two centuries later, our first Roman Catholic president, John F. Kennedy, to assuage any fears of the pope interfering in his presidential decisions, said in 1960, "I believe in an America where the separation of church and state is absolute."

Unfortunately, since the time of Ronald Reagan's presidency, some within the religious right have attempted to influence governmental officials and decisions, attacking people and parties whom they accuse of driving religion from the public square. Because these religious leaders continue to promote the myth that America was founded as a Christian nation, they feel it is appropriate to impose their own rather narrow religious interpretations and agendas on the American public. In the process, this eroding of the separation between church and state is creating serious divisions in our country that threaten the vision of America. Consider, for example, their constant insistence on inserting prayer (the Christian version of course) into our public schools. Such views are directly contrary to the intention of the founding fathers that no religious group should be allowed to enforce its will upon the body politic, as it is being attempted today. All have unalienable rights, and these shall not be abridged.

The truth is that the vision of America enshrined in our founding documents is actually quite consonant with the biblical vision of the prophets, who called the people to do justice and to love mercy. Jesus, too, taught these principles, and he shared with the prophets the vision of the coming kingdom of God—the age of peace and justice and love. The biblical vision is the vision of *shalom*, of peace and wholeness, of God's will for us and for all human beings and for nature itself, that we all can be and have everything that God intends for us. All of these understandings are in keeping with the

American vision. Unlike the religious right's agenda, however, this does not suggest that we are to have a *theocracy* in America—a country "ruled by God" (which means, of course, ruled by the priests who say they speak for God). This is expressly forbidden in the constitution. The impact that people of faith should have on government is to call leaders to be faithful to the vision of liberty and justice for all, and to be concerned for what Jesus called "the least of these": the left out, the forgotten, the persecuted. To do so is to be seriously and thoughtfully patriotic.

It's about compassion

Compassion, not hatred, is a hallmark of true patriotism. Compassion is the foundation on which we build the just society envisioned by our country's founders. The fundamentalist religionists claim that they hold to true morality and family values. In reality, true moral values and true patriotism are to be found when we reach out to give assistance by helping people become productive citizens so that those who have not yet shared in the American dream can become active participants in the promise of America.

In contrast to the hateful invectives often hurled at those whom the religious right accuses of "knee-jerk liberalism," Jesus specifically names some of the compassionate actions that are the signs of those who are entering the kingdom of God. "When I was hungry . . . thirsty . . . a stranger . . . needing clothes, sick . . . in prison" you were there for me. "Whatever you did for the least of these brothers and sisters of mine, you did for me." Interestingly enough, Jesus sends those who have not shared in these values—to "outer darkness!" (Matthew 25:31 ff.) We say to the detractors of this "liberal" morality, "Just what is there about compassion that you don't understand?"

In the aftermath of the destruction of the Gulf Coast and New Orleans by Hurricane Katrina, we saw the stark reality that there are two classes of people in the United States,—the haves and the have-nots. True patriots will strive to pay the price so that the underclass and all those who are denied access to the American dream,—to liberty and justice for all—will share in it. This does not mean promoting a welfare state where people are perpetually on the dole, but it does mean that we will be committed to championing those programs and activities that affirm the constitutional rights of all people to strive for lives of dignity and self-worth. (Please see Chapter 6 for a discussion of such programs and activities.)

The reality is that it is a liberal philosophy of patriotism that has been responsible for the enactment of these sorts of programs. Look at the liberal victories that have been achieved in the past. Laborers won a five day work week and an eight hour day. They worked for job security and pension plans (now being threatened or eliminated). Liberals fought for safe and decent conditions in the work place and for fair and sufficient wages for all, including women (now under attack for both males and females). Social Security was initiated under liberal President Franklin Roosevelt, so that the aged need not live in a state of extreme poverty or destitution (now being threatened). The civil rights movement fought for equal rights for all, most specifically including people of color and those who were not part of the privileged establishment. Liberals—whatever their color—were, and are, deeply involved in this struggle. And, yes, we are also striving for the inclusion of rights for gays and lesbians (now very much under attack). All of these activities are consistent with a fervent desire to work for what is best and noblest in the American dream. Isn't that what patriotism is all about?

Unity in diversity

In addition to compassion, we believe that diversity is also a hallmark of patriotism. Patriotism affirms the diversity that is inherent in our unity. America is a great experiment made up of diverse elements striving to live together in a reconciled way. No other country in the world—ever—has brought together in one place "all the nations of the earth" as we have in the United States. The American experiment is unique in the course of history. We are truly a pluralistic people.

On the Fourth of July, our Independence Day, we celebrate both our diversity as well as our commonality, "one nation, indivisible." We are of different sexes and colors. We come out of different roots, with different languages and cultures. We are from various classes and traditions. We have different religious beliefs, and different stories define us. We all add different gifts to the strengthening of our country. Yet, there is something that unites us that is stronger than that which divides us. For we all share in a common underlying humanity, and we share in a common underlying dream. The Judeo-Christian tradition describes it as being equally "in the image of God."

Each one of us is of infinite worth. This is the American vision. It is totally inconsistent with those who perceive that they are superior to others because others are different. The prophet Amos, in the name of God, condemned those people who felt that because they were the "chosen people", they were superior to all others. "Are you not as the children of the Ethiopians unto me, O Children of Israel, says the Lord? Have I not brought up Israel out of the land of Egypt? And the Philistines from Caphtor, and the Syrians from Kir?" (9:7) In God's eyes, and in the American vision, we are *all* chosen,—"with liberty and justice for all."

Because we are all diverse and yet bound together in a common humanity, America has never really been the "great melting pot" that many people have talked about. Rather, together we are a great mosaic, with each person unique and each culture different. Nevertheless, together we make up a multicultural masterpiece. Sadly, this ideal vision of a diverse yet unified America is blurred by the fact that there is a great difference between the *vision* of America and the *reality* of America. There still is a great gulf between a healthy diversity where we live in reconciled harmony and the factionalism of race, creed, and class that tears apart the fabric of our society. It is this disastrous fragmented diversity that has created many of the injustices in our land and portrays America at its worst. It makes us suspicious, fearful, and prejudiced against each other—against anyone who is not "like us." It is the cause of the neglect of those who live on the social and economic bottom of our society; of the dislike, if not downright hatred, of those who do not share our ethnic, religious, or sexual backgrounds; of those who have differing viewpoints about how to realize the vision of America.

In the midst of these realities, the measure of a true patriot is her or his commitment to the support of policies and programs that not only recognize the benefits of our diversity, but also have as their goal the inclusion of everyone in the promise of the American dream. Patriots are committed to investing in America's people and our environment so that we, and the whole world, will have a sustainable future. Patriots are concerned with "people priorities" rather than the priorities of the powerful and of vested interests. To be committed to these goals is to uphold the untarnished meaning of patriotism.

Holding our leaders responsible

A patriot has the courage to call our leaders to accountability. Patriotism is about keeping the focus on the vision. When that vision is defiled, patriots are willing to have the courage of their convictions and stand in opposition to policies that are undemocratic, unjust, and that do not reflect the high ideals on which this country was founded. Patriots speak out when our basic freedoms are eroded and when our government ignores basic human rights, as for example, in the current administration's apparent policy of condoning torture, as it has done with Iraqi and other prisoners.

If one of the marks of a patriot is to protect and preserve the common good, then patriotic Americans will object to policies that they view as destructive of the common good and of the well-being of future generations. We do not have to look very far to see such policies. Both in Iraq and in the aftermath of Hurricane Katrina, favored companies with ties to the administration have received huge government contracts without competitive bidding. There is incontestable evidence of global warming caused by the release of fossil fuel gasses, and yet there is no strong national policy to control our gluttonous waste. Gargantuan deficit spending is mortgaging our children's children, in the biblical phrase, "unto the third and fourth generation." We are involved in a war that is dubious at best, and in the minds of increasingly many citizens, a war that has done nothing to diminish the threat of terrorism. Indeed, an excellent case could be made that Iraq has become a cauldron of terrorism precisely because we have invaded that country. It is perhaps no exaggeration to state that we are teetering on the precipice of an apocalypse largely of our own making. It is of paramount importance when our country is in danger of losing its moorings that we hold our leaders responsible and work toward moving our country once again in a constructive direction consistent with our founding ideals.

Making a difference

How do patriotic Americans—and that includes liberal and many conservative Americans as well—address these devastating realities and at the same time keep our eyes on the vision of America? How does one act patriotically in facing the challenges of the future that sometimes seem almost insurmountable? Here are some ideas for starters:

- Be informed about the founding vision of our great country and keep focused on that vision.
- Work to elect and vote for leaders who are committed to wise and compassionate policies, and exhibit compassion in the exercise of daily living.
- Speak out for the protection of civil liberties.
- Be prepared to sacrifice and pay the price—and it will undoubtedly be substantial at times—so that others might share in America's promise.
- Remember that our enemy is not other people; our enemies are prejudice, exploitation, and injustice, and the policies that help to feed them.
- Take to heart the words of the prophet Amos: "Take away from me the noise of your hymns, to the melody of your harps I will not listen. But let justice roll down like waters and righteousness like an everflowing stream." (Amos 5:23)

Talking Points

- **There is a difference between patriotism and chauvinism (blindly loyal and aggressive patriotism).**
  Thoughtful patriots understand the complexities involved in our love relationship with our country. Ongoing debate and differences of opinion are essential in the American system. To believe otherwise is to operate with a misguided understanding of patriotism, often referred to as chauvinism. Chauvinism is zealous and aggressive, believing that "God is on our side" and putting blind uncritical faith in one's leaders. Chauvinist beliefs are once again gaining prominence in our society. In defense against this, thoughtful patriots must reclaim the vision on which America was founded.

- **Patriotism should not be based on the mistaken premise that America was founded as a Christian nation.**
  Although there are those who believe that our founding fathers intended for America to be a Christian nation, these viewpoints do not reflect the spirit of the founding fathers who were fearful of religious interference in the rule of law. Instead, they reflect the spirit of Cotton Mather who believed that Americans were people of chosenness and destiny. In reality, the founding fathers were rationalists and deists.

- **Patriotism holds America to the ideals on which it was founded.**
  Embodied in our country's founding documents is the belief that our government is charged with the responsibility to serve the common good. These documents emphasize that *all* people are created equal and have the right to life, liberty, justice, and the pursuit of happiness. Especially germane for our situation today is the constitutional insistence on the separation of church and state. Although the vision of America enshrined in our founding documents is consistent with the biblical

vision of peace and wholeness, it does not advocate a theocracy (a country ruled by God, or the people who say they speak for God) in America.

- **Patriotism is based on compassion rather than hatred.**

  Compassion, not hatred, is the hallmark of true patriotism. It is the foundation on which we build the just society envisioned by our country's founders. The stark reality is that there are two classes of people in the United States—the haves and the have-nots. True patriots will strive to pay the price so that the underclass and all those who are denied access to the American dream of liberty and justice for all will share in it.

- **Patriotism affirms the diversity that is inherent in our unity.**

  America is a great experiment made up of diverse elements striving to live together in a reconciled way. We are truly a pluralistic people, and we all add different gifts to the strengthening of our country. Yet we all share in a common underlying humanity and underlying dream. Sadly, this vision of a diverse yet unified America is not always reflected in reality. One measure of patriotism is a commitment to support the inclusion of all Americans in the promise of the American dream.

- **A true patriot has the courage and the duty to call our leaders to accountability.**

  Patriotism is about keeping the focus on the vision, not on the party or the leader of the moment. When that vision is defiled, patriots are willing to stand in opposition to policies that are unjust and do not reflect the high ideals on which this country was founded. They will object to policies that are destructive of the common good. They address the devastating realities of our times by such actions as becoming informed about the founding vision of our country, working to elect wise and compassionate leaders, being prepared to sacrifice so that others might share in America's promise, and if necessary, being willing to die for a cause that is just and honorable.

3

Ain't Gonna Study War No More

It was President Dwight Eisenhower who, several decades ago, said "I'd like to believe that people in the long run are going to do more to promote peace than our governments. Indeed, I think that people want peace so much that one of these days governments had better get out of the way and let them have it." Yet today, war still is glorified in the name of national interest. Fundamentalistic conservatives selectively interpret "thou shalt not kill" to serve their own narrow anti-abortion agenda, while at the same time, 19-year-old "fetuses" are killed by the thousands, and many times more civilians are slaughtered and dismissed as "collateral damage." What is wrong with this picture? That's what this chapter is all about.

Iraq: a house divided

We in the United States remain divided over the issue of war in general and specifically over the Iraq war. One of the harsh realities of our human existence is war, usually defined as the using of force or armed conflict as a method of addressing disputes. War, for Christians, has been a matter of discussion and debate virtually since the beginning of the Christian era. Historically, and continuing into the present day, society has been conflicted about whether and how war should be waged. Throughout the Christian era, three approaches to war have developed in response to the changing social and political realities of the times—pacifism, holy war, and the just, or justifiable, war. Within our current socio-political context, and especially in light of the conflicts in Iraq and other parts of the Middle East, it seems essential that there be careful deliberation on these various approaches to war, so that people of good will might thoughtfully assess our country's involvement in current and potential situations of conflict.

The war in Iraq has forced a reexamination of the question of under what circumstances a nation goes to war. Although the invasion of Iraq initially had the support of the majority of the United States public, but by no means most of the world's nations, the tide of public opinion has turned as of this writing, with a vast majority of Americans now disapproving of the less-than-truthful reasons for the invasion of Iraq and the way in which this administration has handled the war.

The current administration and many conservatives seem to feel that dissent regarding the Iraq war is unpatriotic. The ubiquitous car tag, "support our troops" seems to implicitly suggest that to be against the war is to abandon our military. Increasing numbers of people are counter-arguing, however, that perhaps the best way to support our troops may be to get them out of harm's way by bringing them home in a planned and orderly fashion, or, if they are to stay, to provide them with the best equipment and supplies necessary for them to do the job.

Much of the current discontent and uneasiness about Iraq has to do with the fact that the reasons for going to war and the prospects for victory have turned out to be less than candid. We were told by the administration that this war was inevitable because it is in the national interest and it is being waged to protect our "national security." The President persistently says that we are fighting terrorists on "their" soil rather than ours. Saddam Hussein, Bush averred, had weapons of mass destruction. Iraq, we were led to believe, played a significant role in the terrorist acts on the World Trade Center on September 11, 2001. Many

Iraqis, it was said, wanted the U.S. to invade Iraq and would welcome our troops with open arms. The war would be over in weeks, the Secretary of Defense said. Now we know that these rationales have turned out to be, if not outright lies, at least considerably less than the total truth. Many Americans now have the uneasy feeling that we are in a quagmire.

At the same time, some on the "religious right" continue to view this war as a holy war, uncritically supporting our involvement in it without considering the morality, or lack thereof, involved with it. One is reminded of the obscene war prayer which Mark Twain sardonically wrote:

> O Lord, we go forth to smite the foe. Help us to tear their soldiers to bloody shreds; help us to cover their smiting fields with the pale forms of their patriot dead; help us to lay waste their humble homes with a hurricane of fire; help us to wring the hearts of their unoffending widows with unavailing grief. For our sakes, who adore thee, Lord, blast their steps, water their way with their tears. (quoted in *The New York Times*, December 7, 1914)

While this "prayer" is obviously an exaggeration, it nevertheless forces us to think about the dangers of not only blindly accepting war as a solution to conflict, but also how easy it is to assume that God is always on our side. How did this uncritical attitude toward war come about? And how can concerned citizens make thoughtful moral judgments about war? In order to answer these questions, at least from a Judeo-Christian standpoint, it is necessary to have a basic understanding of the various approaches to war within the Judeo-Christian tradition.

Pacifism: the early Christian approach

The earliest Christian attitude concerning war was pacifism—opposing any war or violence as a means of settling disputes and refusing to participate in military action. Early Christians lived as Jesus perceived they should, as a "city on a hill," whose light was to shine before others to the glory of God. By their loving and peaceful example, they tried to reflect in their lives what the kingdom of God would finally become. These early Christians sought to emulate Christ by turning the other cheek and practicing what Jesus described in the Sermon on the Mount(Matthew 5:1-12): "Blessed are the peacemakers, for they shall be called the children of God. Blessed are the merciful, for they shall obtain mercy. Blessed are the meek for they shall inherit the earth." By their example they endeavored to stand in vivid contrast to a decadent and inhumane society, and thus to influence the world; to be, as Jesus said, a light to the world. Contemporary and ancient scholars alike agree that the roots of Christianity are planted in pacifism. With regard to more contemporary scholars, all seem to agree that until sometime around 170-180 A.D., Christians were neither involved in warfare nor served as soldiers. (See, for example, R. Bainton, *Christian Attitudes Toward War and Peace*, 1960 and Guy F. Hershberger, *War, Peace, and NonResistance*, 1969, Herald Press: Scottdale, PA).

None of the existing writings of early Christian theologians in the pre-Constantinian era (up to 313 AD) approved of a military career for disciples of Jesus Christ. In fact, many spoke of Jesus' pacifism. Tertullian wrote, "The divine banner and the human banner do not go together, nor the standard of Christ and the standard of the devil. Only without the sword can the Christian wage war: for the Lord has abolished the sword." (*On the Chaplet*, 11-12). Origen wrote, "You cannot demand military service of Christians any more than you can of priests. We do not go forth as soldiers." (*Against Celsus*, VIII.7.3, ca. 240 AD). Justin Martyr wrote, "We ourselves were well conversant with war, murder, and everything evil, but all of us throughout the whole wide earth have traded in our weapons of war. We have exchanged our swords for ploughshares, our spears for farm tools. Now we cultivate the fear of God, justice, kindness to men, faith, and the expectation of the future given to us by the Father himself through his Son Jesus." (*Dialogue with Trypho*, 110.3) Hippolytus (218 AD) states that soldiers who become Christians were not allowed to kill and were required to refuse to obey orders to kill. (*The Apostolic Tradition*, 16)

The Christian church during these first two centuries can be described as a counter-cultural movement, trying to live out the radical ethic of Jesus amid the harsh, often depraved, and hostile realities of Greco-Roman society. Thus, early Christians avoided active participation in secular affairs because it meant having to offer sacrifices to the emperor as a god who was seen as the divine personification of Rome. In this regard, Tertullian also said that judges acting within the Roman system of jurisprudence who wanted to become followers of Christ either had to resign or be rejected by the church.(*The Apostolic Tradition*, 16)

Early Christians refused military service because killing was against the clear teachings of Jesus. It was this stance, as well as their refusal to participate in any capacity that would require them to worship the emperor, that led to their persecution. In the *Acta Martyria*, which might be described as court transcripts from those early days, we read of Christians being interrogated and tortured and finally killed for their faith. Refusal to participate in the system branded them as unpatriotic and enemies of the state. As the population of the empire became more Christian, however, some did serve in the army as long as military service consisted of non-violent police work Many Christians, for instance those who served in the military regiment called the Moorish Legion in the pre-Constantine era, were executed because they would not perform acts of violence, including blood-letting.

This early Christian pacifism, however, could not survive the social and cultural changes that occurred during the age of Emperor Constantine, and by the year 314 AD, the church was actually excommunicating military deserters without any consideration of the motives of the desertion. What caused this decline of pacifist ideals? Emperor Constantine, who at least claimed to be a Christian, initiated these changes first by legalizing Christianity and then by making it the official religion of the Roman empire in 325 A.D. In doing so, Constantine was able to control the church and domesticate Christianity for his purposes.

The once radical counterculture became more like an elite in-house religion. From then on, Christianity's vision of the kingdom of God, under the lordship of Christ, was compromised by the lordship of a Christian Caesar. The church, at least until the demise of Constantine's empire, was under the thumb of the state.

The early pacifist tradition is still reflected in the so-called "peace churches" in the United States, such as Quakers (Society of Friends), Mennonites, and Church of the Brethren. Historically, these "peace church" groups often formed communes in order to consciously live out the Sermon on the Mount, and thus to practice the vision of the kingdom of God apart from worldly affairs. Today, however, most members of peace churches play an active role in promoting peacemaking within secular society. In this way they are following in the tradition of their foremothers and fathers in Civil War days who were involved in the underground railway, smuggling escaped slaves to the north, often as far as Canada. In the midst of a world caught up in the spirit and practice of war, pacifists, or "aggressive peacemakers" as many prefer to be called, continue to promote conflict resolution, seek peaceful alternatives to war, and in countless ways, serve as advocates for peace and justice. They live Jesus' ethic of peace, and, indeed, they have the words of Jesus and early Christian history on their side.

"Holy war:" an oxymoron

It was during the medieval crusades that the concept of the "holy war" evolved within the Christian tradition. Holy wars, far from having any holy attributes, are characterized by a crusading and often blood-thirsty spirit, as devastatingly described in Mark Twain's sardonic war prayer which we quoted above. The idea of holy war was common in the ancient world, and examples of such battles are described in the Hebrew Scriptures, as, for instance, when Joshua and the Hebrew army invaded Canaan, the promised land, attacked and defeated Jericho, and destroyed all human and animal life as a holocaust (a sacrificial or total offering) to God. (Joshua 6:16-21)

This notion of holy war resurfaced within the Christian church of the middle ages at the time when Muslim Turkish armies began to invade Eastern Christian lands. In response, the Eastern Orthodox Church turned to the Western Catholic Church for aid in halting the invaders who had taken over the Holy Land and were in possession of many sites that had become sacred to Christians. It was Helen, the mother of the first Christian emperor, Constantine who, mainly by pious and often faulty guesswork, had identified these sites as places where Jesus was born, lived, performed his acts of ministry, suffered, was crucified, and rose again.

With a rallying cry of *"Deus Volt"* ("God wills it"), freeing these holy sites became the sacred mission of the Western Catholic church in its efforts to raise armies for its crusades against the "infidel." These crusades, or holy wars between the 11th and 14th centuries, were carried out intermittently, with great loss of life. The justification was that it was proper to kill the invaders because not only were they usurpers, but they also believed in a different God, a false god. Crusaders were even granted plenary indulgences by the papacy—the promise that after death, all time in purgatory would be cancelled—so that people could at once attain heaven if they participated in the holy wars. Because of the bloody cruelty and injustice involved, these crusades were largely a shameful blot on the pages of Christian history. They sometimes led to the slaughter of people who were guilty of no other crime than speaking another language or worshiping within a different religious tradition.

Christians, however, were not, and are not, the sole culprits in fostering the crusading spirit. The idea of holy war also applies to the history of Muslim expansion, and it is the attitude and motivation of those involved in terrorist attacks on the West today, waged in the name of *jihad*, or holy war. No matter in what tradition it rears its ugly head, nothing is more fearful—or heinous—than killing in the name of God.

This same crusading spirit has been evident throughout much of the American experience as part of the history of "manifest destiny" in the formation of the United States. It was thought by many that God—or destiny—depending upon one's particular viewpoint, gave us the right to take the land, kill the Native Americans, and live off the backs of the slave system. Of course, much of this attitude was—and still is—motivated by greed and racist imperialism. There remains a strong spirit of holy war among us. Often churches have blessed such wars, claiming that "God is on our side." The German military in World War I had the words, *"Gott mit uns"* ("God with us") written on their belt buckles. Propaganda from both church and state even now would have us believe that our cause is God's because our cause is just. Abraham Lincoln understood that it is not for us to presume to know what the will of God is. When, during the Civil War, Lincoln was depressed by its lack of progress, Secretary of War Stanton attempted to offer comfort by saying, "Mr. Lincoln, God is on our side." Lincoln answered, "Yes, but are we on God's side?" Lincoln's humility is a healthy antidote to the dangers of acting on the idea of "holy war" in which we assume that God is on our side without closely examining whether we are acting on God's side.

"Just war:" when all else fails

Centuries before holy wars were employed by Christendom and the church, St. Augustine had formulated the principles of "just war" in response to the legitimate need to defend society and its institutions from encroaching enemies. As we have seen, pacifism began to decline in the early fourth century, beginning with the conversion to Christianity of the emperor Constantine. When Christianity was finally made the official religion of the Holy Roman Empire, the church found itself faced with the difficult realization that there were occasions when, of necessity, it appeared that war had to be waged. Specifically, Christians had to find some justification for self-defense against the ongoing invasions by the ethnic tribes that had been migrating west over many generations from the steppes of Russia. Thus, it was in the context of needing to take upon itself the responsibility of dealing with wars for the defense of society and its institutions that the early church developed the theory of the just (a better term would be justifiable) war. War, by its very nature, always creates injustice, but the church realized also that there were times when it was possible to justify a given war, knowing that sometimes a lesser violence could avert a greater violence.

St. Augustine, the bishop of Hippo, was the first theologian to address the "just war" concept in a competent, scholarly way, and his writings serve as the classic basis for the just war theory. Augustine argued that for a war to be considered "just," there must be a) a just cause, b) legitimate authority given for the war, and c) right intention, that is, there should be no hidden motives, such as land seizure or perpetration of atrocities. This just war concept wasn't fully developed until after the majority of the crusades—the "holy wars"—had ended. Thomas Aquinas, in the thirteenth century, adapted Augustine's categories to the circumstances of his day, which were characterized by periods of unrest among developing nation-states. He expanded on the question of what constitutes "legitimate authority" when nations or peoples are contemplating war. While Augustine thought that such authority came from God alone, Thomas Aquinas believed that the criterion for judging the legitimacy of a ruler, and that ruler's authority to declare war, was how well the ruler served the common good of his constituents. For this reason, he believed that rebellion would be justified if the people rose as a body against unjust and tyrannical rulers. He also proposed other criteria for entering a war and rules of engagement in the war, which will be discussed in the next section of this chapter.

Thomas Aquinas' theory of the just war was not only accepted by later Roman Catholic theologians, but also by the Protestant reformers and theologians of ensuing generations, with certain elaborations. With the passage of time, Christians came to consider the just war tradition as embodying essential rules of conduct among Christian nations. During the times of colonial conquest by European nations, which was often extremely brutal, theologians and statesmen extended just war norms to the treatment of indigenous peoples who were being forcibly colonized by European nations. By the time of the rise of the modern nation-state in the Middle Ages, the principles of the just war theory had become the standard for western "Christian" nations, in theory at least, if not always in practice. From these developing just war principles were laid the foundations for modern international law regarding war.

When is a war just?

An understanding of the principles of the "just war" is important, not only because they have become foundational for the formulation of modern international law, but also because they can provide moral guidance regarding our involvement as a nation in international disputes. These principles are divided into two categories: 1) the criteria for judging whether resorting to force is justified, and 2) if war is justifiable, the criteria for the regulation of the use of force in conflict.

The criteria for judging whether or not resorting to war is necessary are:

Is the war justifiable? War is only justifiable when it confronts "a real and certain danger." Historically, this meant a defense against aggression on the part of other parties and nations. One question to be asked is whether the results achieved will provide greater opportunities for freedom and justice than if there had been no war. In light of the types of "ethnic cleansing" that have occurred in places like Rwanda-Burundi, the former Yugoslavia, and the Sudan, "humanitarian intervention" has become a new formulation of the criterion for just cause.

Was war declared by a competent authority? The war must be declared and carried out by a legitimate authority having jurisdiction in the matter. Revolutionary uprisings may be sanctioned where there is "manifest long-standing tyranny."

Is the war based on "right intentions?" The war must not be initiated under false pretenses such as when there are hidden motives other than the ones that are publicly stated. These could include stealing a territory, seeking revenge, or pursuing economic domination. This criterion also prohibits intent to commit "unnecessarily destructive acts" and criminal acts such as massacre, rape and pillage.

Can it be shown that going to war is a last resort? War must only be initiated when all possibilities for peaceful arbitration have been exhausted and all other peaceful alternatives have not been successful.

Is there a good probability of success? Is there a reasonable prospect of victory? An indecisive conflict indefinitely prolonged was not considered just, especially if there were dubious objectives to begin with.

After a country has entered into a justifiable war, the following criteria apply for conducting a war:

Non-combatants should be immune from the application of direct force. According to traditional "just war" theory, destructive force in war is only to be applied to those who actively threaten the innocent. Unarmed and non-threatening people are not to be killed. Unfortunately, battles are no longer waged in arenas where the military fight it out in the plain, while civilians watch the proceedings from surrounding hills in relative safety. During the course of the history of war, the killing of the innocent, particularly children, women and the elderly, has dramatically escalated. It is estimated that in World War II, about 45% of the casualties were civilian; in Vietnam, 65%; and in the 1990's, where guerrilla warfare and terrorism were often the method of violence, about 90% of those killed were civilian casualties.

Hostilities should involve no excessive destruction. Small-scale injuries should not be avenged with large-scale devastation. There should be no excessive destruction. An event that happened during World War II provides us with a sad example. When Germany obliterated the English city of Coventry in World War II in a bombing raid, Winston Churchill, the prime minister of England, insisted that the city of Dresden, Germany be equally devastated in aerial attacks as an act of revenge. Both acts were obvious violations of just war principles. Unfortunately, history shows us that with the acceptance of the concept of just war also came the possibility that nations could justify any war deemed in a nation's interest, and principles of moderation in carrying out the war are frequently ignored.

What about Iraq?

We maintain that the Iraq war is not in accordance with the principles of a "just war" or with international law. In our current world situation it remains appropriate for the United States to be informed by the concept of the just war because, even though it has roots in the Christian tradition, this concept has been embraced by most of the nations of the world. The principles of just war are recognized in the United Nations Charter and have been enshrined in international law. It is appropriate, then, to look at the just war criteria in light of the Iraq war.

Can we claim that the cause is justifiable? In our opinion, no convincing case has ever been made by the current administration for the invasion of Iraq. The rationale for entering the war has changed time and again, leading one to the conclusion that the war was declared under false pretenses. President Bush told the American people and the world that we were fighting the perpetrators of 9/11, although evidence available at the time was clear that Saddam was not involved in the plot. The president also said that by fighting in Iraq, we were fighting the terrorists on their home soil. Again, the reality is the opposite. We have created a myriad of new terrorists and alienated the Muslim world, as well as our own allies. Finally he said that Saddam either had, or almost had, weapons of mass destruction, when, in fact, Iraq had none. Given the facts of this situation, how could any of these scenarios possibly provide a justifiable reason to go to war?

Was this war authorized by competent authority? The war was declared without the approval of the United Nations, when, by law, if an outside response to a regional or internal conflict is necessary, the United Nations Security Council stands as the constituted authority. The United States attempted to force the issue before the United Nations with no success. When nations such as France and Germany refused to relent to pressure, they were looked upon by many in the United States as social outcasts. In the name of patriotism, boycotts were urged against French wine, and french fries were for a time renamed "freedom fries" in the congressional restaurant. Only a few nations supported the war. Most of them were indebted to the United States financially and are so small and unknown that many Americans had never heard of them before.

Is this war based on "right intentions?" Given the appearance that the Iraq war was probably initiated under false pretenses, we can also call into question the motivation for the war. When we look behind our involvement in Iraq, other, sometimes sinister, motives present themselves. Obviously, the issue of oil cannot be ignored, especially since the United States is by far the greatest user of oil in the world, and oil is increasingly being depleted.

It is also important to be aware of a long-standing neo-conservative agenda that was developed by men who currently surround President Bush and who favor "American global military, diplomatic and moral leadership" to shape a new century favorable to American principles and interests. They have promoted an ideology of U.S. world domination through the use of force.

Was going to war a last resort? All possibilities for peaceful arbitration were not exhausted. In fact, Saddam was being held successfully at bay with previously existing U.N. sanctions. George H. W. Bush, during the first Iraqi conflict, wisely left Iraqi soil, knowing that remaining in Iraq opened up a source of many unforeseen troubles, which could not be contained. His son, however, chose to invade Iraq before pursuing a more peaceable path to its end, as is evidenced in a recently published memo of the British government.

Is there a good probability of success? The prospect of a satisfactory settlement in Iraq is at best ambiguous. It has become increasingly apparent that we entered Iraq with no concrete plans for victory and that we still have little idea about what would constitute victory or what it might take to ensure success there. It appears that the new constitution, instead of establishing peace, has become a motivating factor for Sunni Muslims to engage in a prolonged civil war. This is due, in part at least, to the fact that they perceive the Kurds and Shiite Muslims as having access to the oil-rich territories in Iraq and the wealth of the land, whereas the Sunnis argue that they do not. It is possible that other Middle Eastern nations may soon become involved in the embroilment on Iraqi soil if civil war becomes full-blown. We may well question whether we still have anything to offer a people in a land that has in so many places been reduced to rubble because of this war. How, in the face of all of this, can the United States guarantee even a limited successful outcome?

Thus, the commencement of the Iraq war cannot be supported under a theory of the just war. Similarly, we have not followed the principles of just war in conducting the Iraq war.

Are non-combatants reasonably immune from the application of direct force? In America, throughout this war we have lived with a blanket of censorship, denied the right to see the return of our own dead and maimed soldiers. There has also been an abysmal wall of visual and audible silence about the impact of the war on the Iraqi people. As of this writing, estimates of Iraqi deaths and maimings range conservatively from over 30,000 to well over 100,000 men, women and children. We call it "collateral damage."

Have hostilities involved excessive destruction? The evils of the Saddam Hussein regime—which were not directed toward the United States—have been avenged by large-scale devastation. Although the U. S. forces began the conflict with massive bombardments to awaken "shock and awe," now we have learned all too sadly that terrorist guerrilla tactics can be more devastating than massive modern weaponry. Nothing of what the United States has wreaked upon the Iraqi people, nor the terrorist nightmare responses, reflect the just war's concept of proportionality. As Robert Kennedy said of Vietnam, so it can be said of Iraq: "We have sent a lion after jungle rot."

Where do we go from here?

Issues of modern warfare, such as guerrilla warfare, terrorism, counterterrorist responses, ethnic cleansing, and nuclear war, were not considered in the development of the just war principles. Such issues call for thoughtful deliberation by citizens and their governments and for incorporation of appropriate responses into international law. In the meantime, however, just war principles continue to offer valid criteria for judging the morality of war.

When governments commit themselves to the just war principles as embodied in international law and in the United Nations Charter, they also commit themselves to precedents established in the past that deal with failures to adhere to these principles. For example, policies and practices consistent with the just war theory were specifically used by the United States and its allies after World War II at the Nuremburg Trials as a rationale for the prosecution, conviction, and often the execution of Nazis for war crimes. A new dimension was also added during these trials, having to do with the refusal to obey immoral orders. This concept was based on the thinking of Hugo Grotius, a theologian and philosopher of the seventeenth century who believed that a moral responsibility supersedes obedience to orders. Specifically, if people are asked to participate in something that contradicts moral responsibility, they are bound by a higher law to disobey. German and Japanese officers and leaders were found guilty at Nuremburg based on this principle.

With the adoption of Grotius' principle into international law, the precedent was established for future leaders and military personnel to be held responsible for war crimes in a court of justice with the right of trial and possible execution. The difficulty for us today lies in the fact that rather than applying the moral principles embodied in the just war theories solely to the aggressions of other nations as we did in World War II, we must also be willing to apply those same criteria to ourselves if need be when our leaders perpetrate the same kind of actions for which we condemned people at Nuremberg. Interestingly, the United States has thus far refused to allow its military personnel to be held accountable at the International Criminal Court at The Hague, Netherlands.

Will the time come when our own leaders will need to be called to account for violations of just war principles? If it does come, will we be willing to endorse such an accounting? The religious community can play an extremely important role in the social order regarding the morality of war, but not in the way that many fundamentalistic conservatives interpret that role. Rather, the religious community must fulfill its prophetic role, speaking out faithfully and calling the state to account whenever it is guilty of injustice or immorality, both in this war and when future wars are contemplated. To be silent against injustice is to be its unpatriotic accomplice. It is our responsibility as patriots and as Christians to ensure that our authorities wield their power in a manner consistent with reason, justice, mercy, and the common good, even at the risk of being called unpatriotic, or even worse, traitors. But, like the early Christians, we must be prepared to pay the price for our prophetic stance and our commitment to a moral and just society. For early Christians, the price was often persecution and even death. Though it may not be as extreme, we too may suffer unpopularity, calumny, and even persecution from those in power for taking positions based on conscience.

Making a difference

Here are a few ideas for ensuring that war is used only as a last resort in settling disputes:

- Admit that war is the worst of all possible solutions to conflict and that pacifism is a noble part of our Christian tradition.
- Join enthusiastically with the few, but increasing number of elected officials in their quest for a reasonable timetable to withdraw from Iraq.
- Question the legitimacy of our current and future leaders by, as St. Thomas Aquinas said, how well they serve the common good of their constituents.
- Promote the development of a "Department of Peace" that would have cabinet-level status.
- Make a case in the public and religious media for the fact that the security of the United States depends largely on the credibility of our international leadership, and not on international bullying.
- Participate in a national and international dialogue encouraging that international laws regarding war include

just war provisions for dealing with issues of modern warfare such as guerrilla warfare, terrorism, counter-terrorist responses, and ethnic cleansing.

- Encourage governmental policies that invest heavily in alleviating the reasons for world unrest as a better strategy than war for increasing our security and improving our international image.

Talking points

- **America is divided over the issue of war in general and specifically over the Iraq war.**

  Society has always been divided about whether and how war should be waged. American attitudes about the Iraq war range from opposition to uneasiness to measured acceptance to unquestioning support. Historically, three approaches to war have evolved: pacifism, holy war, and just war, all three of which are evident in contemporary society.

- **The early Christian Church practiced pacifism.**

  Pacifism—opposing war or violence as a means of settling disputes—was the church's position in the first three centuries of the Christian era. Pacifism, or "aggressive peace-making," has been the stance of "peace churches" throughout their history and continues today.

- **The concept of "holy war" is exemplified in the medieval crusades.**

  The medieval crusades were seen as "holy wars" by the Western church against the Muslim Turks, who occupied the Holy Land and its sacred sites. The crusades are largely considered a blot on Christian history, but the crusading spirit is still very evident today. Muslims have also been involved in *jihad*, or holy war.

- **The need to defend society and its institutions led to formation of a "just war" theory.**

  The just, or justifiable, war theory was developed by St. Augustine and further expanded by Thomas Aquinas and other Christian scholars in response to the fact that there are occasions when, of necessity, war has to be waged. This concept became foundational to modern international law regulating war.

- **The principles of the "just war" offer a moral basis for judging the validity of any war.**

    The following criteria can offer guidance to Christians and all people of good will who are concerned about the morality of any given war: it must a) have a justifiable cause, b) be declared by a legitimate authority, c) not be initiated under false pretenses, d) be used as a last resort, e) have a reasonable prospect of victory, f) only be directed toward those who actively threaten the innocent, and g) involve no excessive destruction.

- **The Iraq war is inconsistent with the "just war" criteria or international law.**

    A comparison of the realities of the Iraq war with these criteria reveals that the morality of this war is in question for the following reasons: a) no convincing case has been made for the invasion of Iraq, b) it did not receive consent from the United Nations, c) people in decisive foreign policy roles may have had hidden motives for the war, d) United Nations sanctions and inspections were not given adequate time to work, e) satisfactory settlement of the war is ambiguous at best, f) ten times more civilians have been killed than military personnel, and g) small scale injuries have been avenged by large scale devastation.

- **Our leadership should be held accountable for failing to uphold the principles embodied in the concept of the "just war."**

    It is our responsibility as patriots and as Christians to ensure that our authorities wield their power in a manner consistent with reason, justice, mercy, and the common good, even at the risk of being called unpatriotic or traitors.

4

Baby Killing? Or An Agonizing Choice?

Life would be so much simpler if only we could all agree on what is "right" and what is "wrong" in any given situation. Unfortunately, life tends to be complicated and messy, and often our ethical choices involve varying shades of gray. Reinhold Niebuhr, the noted ethicist, observed that we are sometimes forced to choose between the immoral and the more immoral. Abortion is one of those agonizing issues that can't simplistically be dismissed as either "pro-life" or "pro-choice." This chapter discusses abortion from the perspective of the Judeo-Christian Scriptures, theological tradition, and the basic principles of reason, love, and justice.

We're talking morality here

An abortion is the premature termination of pregnancy ending in the death of the embryo or fetus. A pregnancy that ends early, but where the embryo or fetus survives to be born as an infant, is instead a premature birth. In medicine, a pregnancy that ends because of an accident or natural causes is qualified as a "spontaneous abortion", while a pregnancy that ends because of deliberate interference with that pregnancy is qualified as an "induced abortion." Spontaneous abortions are also referred to as miscarriages. In common parlance, the term "abortion" is used exclusively for induced abortion. (wikipedia.org)

Technical definitions such as these always seem to make things seem so matter-of-fact. Then real people and real lives and real situations get involved. The precise becomes imprecise, the simple becomes complex, the decisions are blended with indecision. It is further complicated by the reality that different groups define pregnancy and abortion-related terms differently. This often makes even the most elementary communication very difficult. It is compounded by the likelihood that even within the Christian faith, the language spoken and terms used vary diametrically in many cases. Add to that the medical professionals who use still another language, and the possibilities for confusion and disagreement become almost limitless. In spite of all the areas of disagreement on this important issue, the one thing that virtually all agree upon is that abortion is a moral issue as well as a medical and political one. It speaks to our sense of what is good and bad, right and wrong, and that makes it a moral issue.

Abortion is one of the most contentious of all the issues of concern in our current political-religious climate. It has literally polarized our society, torn between protection of the rights of the fetus and the protection of the rights of the woman. The anti-abortionist will say, "What is there about 'you shall not kill' that you don't understand?" The answer to that question, however, is in reality incredibly difficult and complicated, because our society is in many ways a killing field.

Choices of life or death are made every day. For example, most states have chosen to legalize capital punishment, although in the state of Illinois, studies have concluded that there may have been many innocent people who have been on death row, and only the recent science of DNA testing has kept a number of them from execution. We can't help but wonder how many innocent persons have been killed by capital punishment? How many in Texas? How many in the rest of the United States?

War is another example. As discussed in the previous chapter, war is so commonplace in today's world that the morality of it is hardly brought into question, at least by those who consider themselves "patriots." It seems that it is simply enough to claim that war is in the national interest without even bothering to question its morality. Our government seems reluctant to inform us of the number of innocent civilians in Iraq who have been killed as a result of the fighting, preferring to refer to them as "collateral damage." The irony is that many people who are avidly anti-abortion are also heartily pro-war and pro-death penalty.

Making decisions about who lives and who dies are a part of our daily lives, whether we acknowledge it or not. Triage nurses in emergency situations are constantly required to make choices about who to save and who to let die. It's part of the job. And we passively kill people daily through neglect because of crushing poverty and lack of medical insurance for over 40 million Americans. The inundation of New Orleans, because of obvious and blatant failure to strengthen the levees that held back the lake and the sea, could be viewed as murder by neglect. The Army Corps of Engineers had long said that New Orleans might not survive more than a stage three hurricane.

The late Cardinal Joseph Bernardin of Chicago said that the taking of life should be viewed as a seamless garment, meaning that if we are against abortion, we must equally be against the death penalty and nuclear war, as two examples. Although many people are incensed over abortion, they often become blind to other issues of life and death once those fetuses are born and grow and mature in conditions of poverty unfit for civilized humanity. Yes, what part of "you shall not kill" don't we understand?

Does the Bible have all of the answers?

We believe that the issue of abortion can be informed by, but not solely settled by, the Bible or theological authority. Christians turn to their Bibles for ethical guidance, but biblical interpretation can be a highly subjective and culture-bound enterprise. The ancient Mediterranean culture, for example, operated with different world understandings than we do today. Life in ancient Israel was patriarchal, with women playing a subservient role. Life was fragile and short and the propagation of family and people was paramount. Families wanted and prayed for many children, particularly for male heirs. It is no wonder that neither the Old nor the New Testament specifically address the matter of abortion. It simply wasn't an issue, even though it apparently was widely practiced during those times. (See, for example, Roy Bowen Ward, *"Is the Fetus a Person?" at: http://www.rcrc.org/religion/es2/comp.html).*

Part of the basis for disagreement between conservatives and liberals about abortion has to do with differing ways of interpreting the Bible. It is important to remember that the Bible is made up of numerous books written on many subjects over a long period of time. Moderate or liberal Christians recognize that not all passages are of equal value. Many passages of Scripture soar with poetic beauty and meaning, such as many of the Psalms and Jesus' Sermon on the Mount. Others, however, can be quite shocking. For instance, in early biblical writings, as for example in the story of the destruction of Jericho (Joshua 6), God ostensibly calls for "holy war" where inhabitants were to be killed to the last man, woman, child, and animal. Again, in Deuteronomy 21:18-21 we are told that rebellious sons who defied their parents were to be stoned to death. Such passages, if taken literally, reflect a code of ethics that certainly wouldn't be acceptable in modern Western society and that many of us would find inconsistent with Christian faith and values.

Many fundamentalistic conservatives, however, turn the Bible into a book of laws that they selectively use to enforce their particular biases. On the other hand, most centrist and evangelical churches interpret the Bible in terms of the love of God which is expressed in the gospel message of Jesus Christ. That message says that the greatest commandment is love; all else is subject to this. Combing the Bible for "proof passages," as some people do, can be a risky enterprise. If one has a predisposition on any subject, usually one can find some passage or another to support almost any position, as for example slavery and the subordination of women, including the denial of women's suffrage.

What, then, are some of the biblical passages that are used to justify the prohibition of abortion? Some have argued that abortion (or the issue of birth control) is condemned in Scripture because of the strange story of Onan in Genesis 38:7-10. According to ancient Jewish law, there was a practice called "levirate marriage." This law said that if a man died without male descendants, the widow of the man was to be married to a brother of the deceased. The first son of this new marriage was then considered to be the son of the deceased brother, so that he was reckoned to have given birth to a male heir.

Genesis 38 tells us that when Er, the first-born son of Judah died, Judah told his son, Onan, to have sexual intercourse with Tamar, Er's widow, so that she might have a son who could be accounted as Er's offspring. Deciding to "have his cake and eat it too," Onan had intercourse with Tamar. Since, however, a subsequent child would not be considered Onan's, at the moment of climax he practiced *coitus interruptus*, spilling his semen on the ground. Thereupon, according to the story, since what he did was wicked in the Lord's sight, God killed him. Pope Pius XI in his encyclical *Casti Connubii* (1930) used this passage to argue that birth control constitutes abortion and that all abortion is sin. Scholars, however, including Vatican scholars, agree that this particular story is simply a condemnation against refusing to fulfill the duties of levirate marriage, and it would be improper biblical scholarship to interpret it in any other way. Thus, in spite of the papal interpretation, this passage does not address either the issue of birth control or of abortion.

While the Bible does not specifically mention abortion, certainly the Scriptures promote respect for all human life. God is the creator and what God creates is good. What is more, Genesis tells us that God created women and men in God's image. (Gen. 1:26-27) This hardly suggests that we look like God, but that we have god-like qualities. Psalm 139, a wonderful hymn of praise for God's continual creative presence in life, states that God created our inmost being and knit us together in our mother's womb. (Psalm 139 v. 13) We are called to have reverence for human life and for all of the creation that God made and continues to uphold. This reality is constantly before the eyes of the person of faith. Whether a fetus is fully human or potentially human, it is nevertheless God's creation, and it is precious. We must remain mindful of this in our discussions about abortion—and also equally mindful of the humanity and preciousness of women and of those whose views may differ from ours.

When does a human life begin?

Much of the argument about abortion today centers around the issue of when the fetus becomes human. It may be helpful as we begin this discussion to define two related concepts. The first is *human life* which is generally defined as any living form or thing that has DNA from the species *homo sapiens*. This includes an ovum, spermatozoon, zygote, embryo, fetus, and newborn. It also includes an infant, child, adult, or the aged. Additionally, however, human life also includes such things as a lung cancer cell, a hair follicle, and a skin scraping. Some forms of human life, like ova and spermatozoa, are generally considered to have little or no independent value. Others, like a newborn or infant, are generally considered to be extremely valuable, and their life is important to preserve. The second term is *human person*, which is ordinarily defined as any form of human life that is also considered to be an individual, be that man, woman, or child, and thereby has civil rights, including the right to life. There is a societal consensus that a newborn is a human person. People, however, disagree about whether a zygote, an embryo, or a fetus is a human person, based on their differing opinions about the stage at which human life becomes *a human person*. This, then, is a core disagreement that drives the abortion controversy—and Scripture does not definitively settle this issue.

As we have noted earlier, the commandment, "Thou shalt not kill," which is directed against the killing of persons, has been used as a categorical condemnation of abortion. Scripture, however, is rather ambiguous about the status of the fetus. For example, Exodus 21:22f states that if men who are fighting hit a pregnant woman and she has a miscarriage, that is, the fetus is killed, the perpetrator is not to be charged with murder, but is to be fined. If, however, there is serious injury to the woman or she dies, the perpetrator will be put to death, following the principle of "a life for a life." Laws such as these were considered to be God's laws. This particular text suggests that the pre-born fetus was not perceived as being the same as a human being. Potentially human, yes, but not fully human, and the law against killing does not have the same penalty or seriousness. But this is playing the "proof passage" game. Nevertheless, many of the people who argue for abolition of abortion continue to make their judgments based on highly selective passages such as these.

What about Christian tradition?

Early church teachings, likewise, do not offer absolute clarity about the status of the fetus as a human being. The early church operated in a historical context quite different from ours today. It was a counter-cultural community of believers reacting against the non-Christian culture of the Roman Empire. In that historical context, Christians, as defenders of the faith, and in spite of dreadful persecution from Rome, absolutely and unconditionally obeyed the commandments not to kill and to have no other gods. Church fathers clearly spoke against abortion as killing. The ancient Greco-Roman world not only practiced abortion, but also infanticide if the child was unwanted, or malformed, or if the child was a girl. While objecting to all of these forms of infanticide, these early Christian writers objected equally to Christians participating in war as soldiers or actively participating in the governance of the Roman state, which required that the emperor be worshipped as god. Still, many today will appeal to the early church's position on abortion and ignore the commandment not to kill in other circumstances. And today we certainly seem to be cavalier about God's commandment to "have no other gods." In our materialistic society, where money, power, and prestige become the ultimate gods in the lives of many of us, we constantly break that commandment, because our god is whatever is most important in our lives.

Perhaps the greatest fathers in the western church were Saint Augustine (354-430) and Saint Thomas Aquinas (1225-1274). Augustine, in the fifth century, condemned abortion, but not because of the life status of the fetus. Rather, he condemned it because it meant that the sexual act was used for something other than procreation, which Augustine believed was the one and only purpose for the sexual act. (St. Augustine, *De nuptiis et concupiscentia,* 1.15.17 [CSEL 42.229-230] It should be noted, however, that in his writings he also and equally condemned sex after menopause, during infertile periods, and during pregnancy. Church authorities in their wisdom removed such bans long ago. When it came to the question of when the fetus becomes a person, Augustine confessed to being agnostic, not knowing what to believe or not to believe.

St. Thomas Aquinas, in the 13th century, is recognized to this day by many as the standard authority for theology in the Roman Catholic Church. Although Thomas opposed abortion, he differentiated between the seriousness of early and late abortion. He believed that the soul was infused into the body, but he could only guess at what point in the pregnancy this happened. He did not think that it took place at fertilization. He maintained that the sin in abortion was not homicide unless the fetus was "ensouled," and thus became a human being. It was his position that the fetus was first given a vegetative soul, then an animal soul, and then when the body was fully developed, it became a rational soul, in other words, a human being. The Council of Vienne, influential to this day in Catholic teaching, affirmed the conception of humans as set forth by Thomas Aquinas. This theory was and is called the theory of delayed hominization (the process of becoming human.) It remains the most consistent theme and thread throughout Catholic church history on abortion. (Joseph F. Donceel, S.J., "Immediate Animation and Delayed Hominization," *Theological Studies*, vols. 1 & 2. New York: Columbia University Press, 1970, pp. 86-88.)

It is of much more recent vintage that the Roman Catholic Church has insisted that all abortion is infanticide and ruled that birth control is a form of incipient infanticide. Pope Pius IX completely ignored the teaching and concept of hominization and the thought of Thomas Aquinas when he wrote *Apostolicae Sedis* in 1869. In it he said that excommunication was the required penalty for abortion at any stage of pregnancy. He was also the first to say that all abortion was homicide. His statement was the first implicit endorsement of "immediate hominization." (*Actae Sanctae Sedis*, 5:298)

In summary, the Bible and the Christian tradition hold to a deep reverence for all human life, but there is hardly unanimity of opinion within the Bible and among church fathers about the humanity of the fetus, or even for reasons why abortion is not accepted. Yet, some religious fundamentalists of today continue to insist that their tunnel-vision version of what God thinks on this issue is what the laws of this country should reflect. It would seem to be the height of arrogance for people to assume that only they are privy to what is really in the mind of God.

The role of love, human reason, and justice

It is evident that for the informed person of faith, abortion is a serious and highly complex issue, and certainly one with religious implications. However, we live in a secular society, not a religious state. It must be emphasized, as Reinhold Niebuhr stressed, that in a pluralistic democratic society, we may be personally informed by our spirituality, but we cannot bind society as a whole to our personal religious convictions.

For liberal Christians, and for all Christians in theory, love is foundational to our actions. As was stated in the introduction, Niebuhr believed that *agape*, the love of God as shown to us in Jesus Christ, is that kind of love that is always our ideal. In a secular, diverse, and democratic society, however, we are forced to make compromises. This occurs both because of the reality of human sinfulness and because of the necessity of equal justice under law, which often calls for arbitration, compromise, and less than ideal outcomes. Thus, what Niebuhr calls the "middle axiom" (showing love by seeking and doing justice), is often not simply a matter of black and white issues, but involves varying shades of gray. According to Niebuhr, persons of faith must live with the reality of a less-than-perfect ethic of compromise if they are to be active participants in our pluralistic, democratic society.

John Danforth, former senator, United States representative to the United Nations, and moderate Republican, in a recent column in the *New York Times*, demonstrates that principle of the "middle axiom." He says that the difference between moderate and conservative Christians concerns the extent to which government should, or even can, translate religious beliefs into the laws of the state. All Christians have a right to bring their values to bear in politics, Danforth states, but while conservatives think that they alone know God's truth and want to translate that into law, moderates acknowledge the limitations of human beings and believe that the only absolute standard of behavior is the commandment to love our neighbors as ourselves. This commandment takes precedence when it conflicts with laws and has an impact on all sorts of complicated and ambiguous issues in our society. He concludes by saying that by following a Lord who cited love of God and love of neighbor, we reject a political agenda that displaces love. (cf John Danforth, "Onward Moderate Christian Soldiers," *New York Times* Op-Ed, June, 2005)

Natural reason should also be a part of Christian ethical deliberations on abortion. The human intellect is a wonderful gift of a God, who expects us to use it to bring about a just and equitable society. The knowledge provided by the disciplines of philosophy, ethics, the related sciences, and medicine can all be used as we address the related questions about abortion. Even within these disciplines, however, people of good intentions and with good information have interpreted evidence from natural sources in different ways. A consensus has simply not developed with regard to the complexities of abortion generally, and the question of when human life begins specifically. There still is great need for civil, rational discussion on abortion within the public arena. A recent editorial in the *Christian Century*, hardly perceived as a conservative journal, thoughtfully discussed Roe vs. Wade. While not suggesting that legalized abortion be rescinded, it argued that the Supreme Court decision should be reviewed because, in the opinion of the editors, the decision requires refinement in its legal reasoning.

Any rational discussion on abortion will also take into account our commitment as Americans and as Christians to the principle of equal justice under law, and that makes for ambiguity. The protection of the fetus must be weighed against the mother's well-being or the circumstances surrounding the situation. While the rights of the fetus are an important part of the conversation, so are the rights of the mother. Certainly the mother has not sacrificed her right to free personhood. The specific circumstances will necessarily play a significant role in the ethical decision either to abort or bring the infant to full term.

No easy answers

There are no easy answers in ethical decision making. Respect for the rights and liberties of everyone—the parents and the unborn child—may call for decisions that recognize the uncertainties involved. Being the imperfect people that we are, it is hardly surprising that there is no unanimity among people of good will over the issue of abortion. The dividing lines are not vertical, but horizontal, and ethical opinions range across the spectrum. Some hold to an absolutist view, that abortion is morally wrong in all circumstances. Others say that abortion may be permissible under a limited number of specific conditions. Still others maintain that abortion is a decision to be made by the woman alone.

People who leave the door ajar on the abortion issue are by no means only liberals. Not all conservatives want to be judged by the positions of the extreme right. Equally, not all liberals want to be judged by the standards of the extreme left. Frankly, many liberals are uncomfortable with talk of "abortion on demand," just as many conservatives do not embrace the absolute that abortion is morally wrong in all circumstances. The realities of abortion often encompass great human pain and extreme conditions. On this issue and many others, we are informed by Scripture and theological tradition, but we cannot categorically force our religious agenda on a pluralistic, democratic and, to a great extent, secular society. As Christians, we address ethical issues in our own lives from the standpoint of our own faith. However, we participate in the public forum with the agenda with which our society is familiar, namely, using our voices to encourage that we all be informed by the basic principles of human reason, love, and justice.

Some real-life scenarios

The authors of this book have been involved in ministry with people for many decades. Often these people are in deep anguish and highly vulnerable when faced with a pregnancy which highly complicates life, even to the point that a balanced, happy life might no longer be possible. We will share a couple of scenarios to make the dilemmas more real.

Martha and Bill are a couple in their early thirties who are committed to their faith and life in the church. Martha is a dentist and Bill is a regional sales manager who travels a lot. Martha is now in the early stages of an unplanned pregnancy. They have one healthy two year old, but tests have shown that their expected child will be born with serious abnormalities. The prognosis for the child will be a shortened life with huge medical bills. Martha and Bill are considering abortion. They come to you as a professional for counseling. How will you respond?

Mary is a wife and mother of 39 years. Her daughter is in her early teens. She discovers that she is in an early stage of pregnancy. Soon thereafter, she discovers that she has advanced liver cancer. She cannot care for a child even if she comes to full term, and the doctors tell her that it is doubtful if she will live that long. Mary becomes suicidal and hands her pastor her own planned funeral liturgy, to be used after her self-inflicted death. The pastor arranges to have her forcibly placed in a psychiatric ward in hopes that the suicidal depression will pass. She can only be held for a short period against her will, but when she comes home, she is so touched that someone truly cared enough for her to act decisively, that she decides not to kill herself. She does say that she must have an abortion. How will you respond?

Julie is very poor, and having been raised with little nurturing, has had several children out of wedlock. She is pregnant again and desperate; she cannot handle another child. She gets an abortion, but is conscience stricken and depressed. She comes to you for counseling. How will you respond?

A late middle-aged mother discovers that her mentally challenged daughter has become pregnant by a mentally challenged boy at the shelter where the daughter works during the day. The fetus is destined to be mentally challenged as well. The mother comes to you in great agitation and says that her daughter must have an abortion immediately. How will you respond?

Ethical decision-making is hard work

We recognize that our moral deliberations must address complex questions. For example, how do we balance the rights of the mother and the rights of the fetus? What are the ambiguities involved? What are the possible alternatives? What might be the consequences of each alternative? How might your own experience affect your deliberation? Does Scripture offer guidance? What can we learn from science? What is reasonable and just? What is merciful? What is the role of grace and forgiveness for healing in otherwise seemingly untenable circumstances? It is easy to make theoretical value judgments, but when anguished people are overwhelmed with the knotty, often painful events in life, a sense of humility on our part denies easy answers.

Again the point must be stressed: if a person of faith feels personally bound to his/her set of values, do we have the right to coerce the rest of a diverse democratic society to comply with those positions? Christian realists say no.

Making a difference

Because liberal Christians believe that love is in reality an action word, here are some suggested responses that liberals and other people of good will can undertake to diminish the need for abortions in our society:

- To help reduce the approximately one million abortions a year in the USA, advocate for planned parenthood, health care, and child care that could reduce the economic impact on the decisions of many poor women to have an abortion.
- Ensure that our public officials work to improve the incomes and working conditions for all women, but particularly for poor women.
- Make adoptions easier and sexual abuse much more difficult.
- Increase and improve teenage sex and values education as a means of reducing teenage pregnancy.
- Encourage thoughtful and civil discussions on abortion in your faith community.
- Advocate for pro-family policies that promote the wellbeing of all children.

Talking Points

- **Abortion is a moral issue.** Abortion speaks to issues that address what is good and bad, right and wrong, and that makes it a moral issue. Our society makes choices of life or death every day, for example, in the contexts of war, the death penalty, and neglect of the vulnerable. With all of these issues, how do we sort out when 'you shall not kill' does and does not apply?
- **The issue of abortion can be informed by, but not solely settled by, the Bible or theological authority.** The Bible does not specifically address the matter of abortion. Often disagreements about abortion have to do with differing

ways of interpreting the Bible. Some use the Bible as a book of laws. Others interpret the Bible in terms of the love of God and Jesus' message of love. Throughout the Scriptures, however, we are called to have reverence for life.

- **Much of the abortion argument centers around when the fetus becomes human.** It is helpful to distinguish between *human life* and a *human person*. There are differing opinions about when human life becomes a human person. The status of the fetus in Scripture is ambiguous. Among early church fathers there is no unanimity of opinion about the humanity of the fetus or why abortion is not accepted.

- **Opinions related to abortion are also influenced by basic principles of human reason, love, and justice.** Because we live in a secular society, we may be personally informed by our spirituality, but we can't bind all of society to our personal religious convictions. For Christians, love is foundational to our actions. Knowledge provided by the disciplines of philosophy, ethics and the sciences also informs our understandings.

- **Ethical decisions about abortion must recognize the complexities and ambiguities involved.** There is no unanimity of opinion on the issue of abortion, whether among liberals or conservatives. While it is easy to make theoretical value judgments, when hurting and vulnerable people are involved, making an ethical decision is difficult work. Our moral deliberations must address complex questions.

5

Gays, God, and the Gospel

Jesus says a lot about people who are guilty of injustice and oppression. But not once does Jesus mention homosexuality. Nowhere does the Bible condemn people of the same sex living together in a loving relationship. What do the Bible and science really say about homosexuality? And how does this relate to the healing of society? That's the topic of discussion in this chapter.

The Bible and what's happening now

American society and its churches are in ferment over the issue of gays and lesbians, same-sex unions and marriage. Many religious fundamentalists and other social conservatives tend to accuse liberals of having a "homosexual agenda," and of destroying "family values." A whole bloc in our society wants a constitutional amendment to forbid same-sex marriage. Since this is primarily the position of outraged fundamentalist Christians, we must therefore deal with the issue of homosexuality in Christian categories. We will not do this simply by explicating biblical texts alone or reconstructing what later tradition says. To apply the Christian message to today involves dialogue between our tradition and our experience, including the insights and discoveries of science. Fundamentalists tend to be mired in ancient history and have no intention of being reconciled with the sciences. This is obvious, for instance, in the current controversy over evolution versus creation and "intelligent design."

Mainline church denominations, however, see themselves as having a mediating function. Their primary concern is to relate the good news of the message of Jesus so that it speaks with relevance to the society which they are addressing. The task is to struggle with how the "there and the then" of the biblical record gives insight to what the Spirit is saying in the here and the now. Frankly, this approach is quite contrary to those who stress the unchanging nature of the Bible and discount the implications of scientific discovery and the disciplines of learning. We of the mainstream, however, filter the difficult and archaic biblical texts through the lens of love expressed in Jesus Christ. Hopefully we have the humility that we are learners as well as teachers in our dialogue with our complex and ever-evolving world.

The Bible isn't static

Before we look at the biblical texts themselves, a few general comments are in order. Although all Christians believe that there are certainly eternal Scriptural truths, if we turn the Bible into a manual of "do's" and "don'ts" reflecting the world picture of ancient cultures, we easily fall into the trap of idolatry, binding ourselves to the letter of Scripture and ancient history and culture, and letting that take precedence over the Spirit of God who is still speaking today.

Biblical statements must be seen in their context. What God demands in one situation is sometimes overturned in another. For instance, Deuteronomy 23:1-8 says that no emasculated person or foreigner should enter the worshiping assembly. Nevertheless, Isaiah 56:3-8 overrules this; eunuchs and aliens are welcomed within the worshiping community. So also, Jesus in his teachings and ministry frequently overrules Old Testament laws. Thus there is change reflected within Scripture itself. Additionally, as will be evident later, subjective opinions reflected in translations from the original language, as well as outright mistranslations, have always played a role in biblical interpretation and misinterpretation.

What is more, there is not only one voice reflected in Scripture. The Bible was written and shaped over a period of many centuries. The texts reflect changing points of view in different circumstances. For instance, as we have seen in the chapter on war, early Old Testament passages call for "holy war," killing the enemy to the last man women, child and animal. This was perceived as the will of God. Later on, in the book of Isaiah, however, the vision of the new creation is one of peace where people won't learn war anymore. Swords will be beaten into farming implements, "and a little child shall lead them."

Many fundamentalistic Christians use such terms as the "order of creation" and "Christian anthropology" to insist that there is no variance in the Creator's intent from the very beginning to the present, and therefore the order of things is unchangeable and eternally normative for society. So they use ancient texts as though they are eternally binding, and often as instruments of oppression, justifying the subjugation of women, caste and class discrimination, and racial superiority. It has been argued in the course of much of history that these oppressed states correspond with the order of things, and rather obscure biblical texts have been marshaled as evidence. Such arguments were used to enforce *apartheid* in South Africa, and slavery, racial segregation and subjugation in the United States.

This same "order of creation" and "Christian anthropology" argument has been used against homosexuals as well. Homosexuality, it is argued, is rebellion against the intention of the Creator, who, ostensibly, intended sex to occur only between man and woman. To the contrary, however, creation is not a finished product or a static condition. Instead, the ancient creation story in the first chapter of Genesis is dynamic. God is drawing order out of chaos. Realities in the movement of creation, the passage of time and change in cultural circumstances may alter the nature of law in a given time, for God is moving in the world and in history, and that movement changes the nature of things. For instance, we can all agree that the earth revolves around the sun, which contradicts the geocentric understanding of things as they are reflected in Scripture and the ancient world. The theories of Darwin and Freud also demand serious reconsideration of long-held worldviews reflected in the Bible and the ancient world. Therefore, to interpret the creation account as an indictment against homosexuality is to read a lot more into the text than is warranted and ignores the dynamic and changing nature of Scripture.

What do the Hebrew Scriptures really say?

Doesn't the Bible say that homosexual activity is a sin? Can we be faithful Christians and also be supportive of gays and lesbians? You may be surprised to learn that there are only a handful of passages in all of Scripture that deal directly with homosexual activity. Let us first take a look at the various passages in the Old Testament that are generally cited as condemnation of homosexuality to discover what they may—or may not—say on the subject of homosexual practice. As an initial point, it must be stressed that the recovery of the precise meaning of ancient words can be very difficult and at times impossible. When an issue is controversial, such as with homosexuality, people often read their own views and biases into the ancient texts, rather than extracting the meaning from the text itself.

Genesis 19—The story of Sodom—The most influential account that is seen as condemning homosexuality in the Hebrew Scriptures is the story of Sodom in Genesis 19. A purely homosexual-focused interpretation, rather than a more general interpretation, however, is relatively recent. Briefly, the story is this. As two angelic strangers approach the gates of Sodom, Lot, the nephew of the patriarch Abraham who now lives there, extends the ancient obligation of hospitality to the strangers and invites them to spend the night in his home. Thereupon, we are told that every last man in the city surrounds Lot's house. This mob of men, reflecting an egregiously inhospitable spirit, calls to Lot, "Where are the men who came to you tonight? Bring them out to us, so that we may know them" (Gen. 19:2 NRSV). Here, the word "know" denotes sexual intercourse. Lot pleads with them not to do this terrible thing and offers his two virgin daughters for them to brutalize in whatever way they may wish. The crowd responds, "This fellow came here as an alien, and he would play the judge? Now we will deal worse with you than with them." When they try to break the door down, all of the men of the city are miraculously struck blind. The angels drag Lot and his family from Sodom and God rains brimstone and fire upon the city, God's ultimate act of judgment.

To refer to the "sin of Sodom" as merely the intent to indulge in homosexual activity is seriously to abuse the point of the story. This is no act of mutuality between consenting adults. It is intended gang rape, an act of violent inhospitality, the ultimate abuse of the "stranger in the gate."

The fact that Lot would offer his daughters to be gang raped in place of his guests suggests many things. It points to the relatively low value placed on women that such a crime could even be suggested. If Lot would fail in his obligation of hospitality, the shame would be so great that it would be preferable for him to give over his own daughters to be violated. Also, the sexual penetration of women was within the cultural understanding of the role of women, but for a man it was an unacceptable act of violence. There are other references in ancient literature and archeological evidence that male intercourse was used as a means of domination. It was a common practice in biblical times for homosexual rape to be practiced by conquerors to brutalize, degrade, and assert dominance and control over the vanquished. *This is the sin of Sodom!* To refer to a "sodomite" as simply one who engages in homosexual activity is a historical and interpretative error.

It is of interest to note that whenever there is reference to Sodom in the Scriptures, there are varying understandings of its sin. For instance, Isaiah says that Sodom's sin was lack of justice (Is. 1:10; 3:9). Jeremiah accuses Sodom of adultery, lying, and unrepentance (Jer. 23:14). Ezekiel says that Sodom's sin was pride, gluttony, and prosperous ease (Ezek. 6:49). Other sins are mentioned as well, including idolatry. Nowhere, however, is Sodom condemned for homosexual practice.

In the New Testament, Jesus refers to Sodom in the context of possible inhospitality to his disciples, whom he is sending out on a missionary journey. He says that if townspeople are inhospitable to his disciples, it will be better for Sodom in the day of judgment than for those who turn the disciples away (Matt. 10:14-15; Luke 10:10-12).

Deuteronomy 23:17 and I Kings 14:24, 5:12, etc.—Whore and sodomite? Or holy man and holy woman? It is easy to operate with mistaken or incorrect translations, and once these mistranslations find their way into print, the errors often continue in ensuing translations. This is the case in Deuteronomy 23:17f and similar passages in the books of Kings. The King James Version, which influenced many later translations, renders the passage as: "There shall be no whore of the daughters of Israel, nor a *sodomite* of the sons of Israel." Thus, this has been perceived as an attack on male homosexual activity.

In reality, the Hebrew word *qadesh* and the feminine form *qadeshah* mean "holy man" and "holy woman" respectively, here translated as "sodomite" and "whore." Both terms may refer to sacred prostitution, and Old Testament Scriptures heartily condemn such cultic sexual activity. Through the "sympathetic magic" of sexual intercourse, followers of these religions believed that the gods were influenced to engage in sexual activity themselves, which then triggered the processes of fertility in agriculture, animals, and humans. However, this does not connote homosexual activity, as the translation *sodomite* suggests. *Heterosexual activity* was the function of cultic practices in fertility religions. Homosexual activity would have been counterproductive to the purposes of fertility rites. The same equally applies to similar references in I and II Kings. Mistranslations and misconceptions have a way of propagating themselves.

*Leviticus 18:22; 20:13—the "Holiness Code"—*There are two passages in Leviticus that condemn male homosexual acts. "You shall not lie with a male as with a woman; both of them have committed an abomination" (Lev. 18:22 NRSV); and "If a man lies with a man as with a woman, both of them have committed an abomination; they shall be put to death; there blood is upon them" (Lev. 20:13 NRSV) These commands are a part of a collection of laws in Leviticus 17-26 called the Holiness Code because of the frequent repetition, "You shall be holy to me; for I the Lord am holy, and I have separated you from other peoples to be mine" (e.g. Lev. 20:26 NRSV).

The Holiness Code condemns any blending or crossing of lines of categories within creation. Therefore, one would not plant two different kinds of seeds in the same field, or wear a garment made of two different kinds of material (Lev. 20:12). A woman is unclean during menstruation, therefore there should be no contact with her (15:19-24). Eating unclean animals is condemned, ranging from pigs to shellfish (11:2-12). If one had a defect of the eyes he should not approach the altar of God (21:20). Males could not trim hair around the temples (19:27). The death penalty applied to a whole range of things, from cursing one's parents (20:9) to marrying one's half sister (18:6-18), even though Abraham and Sarah, the forebears of the Hebrew people, were half-sister and brother. No one could eat anything with blood in it (17:10-11). It is necessary that these commands in regard to homosexual activity be seen within the totality of the context of the Holiness Code. In the light of all of these rather strange mandates in the Holiness Code, one wonders why for fundamentalist Christians the two passages that may refer to homosexual activity are considered so crucial when the rest of the code, such as killing a child for cursing one's parents and wearing extended sideburns are not taken with the same seriousness. The Holiness Code doesn't rank the seriousness of the prohibitions included within it. Obviously, from the above examples, the truth of the matter is that we cannot assume that the Holiness Code in its entirety is binding upon God's people today.

And the New Testament?

What *does* still apply for us today, and why does it still apply? The New Testament church dealt with this knotty question forthrightly at the Apostolic Council in Jerusalem (ca. 49 A.D.), which dismissed the burden of many Old Testament laws.

James, the brother of Jesus, who was the head of the church in Jerusalem, in consultation with the other apostles, concluded, "Therefore I have reached the decision that we should not trouble those Gentiles who are turning to God, but we should write them to abstain only from things polluted by idols and from fornication and from whatever has been strangled and from blood" (Acts 15:19-20). The Apostolic Council decided that gentiles are not to be unduly bound, while the sensitivities of Jewish Christians should be respected. So we see that the New Testament, in changing cultural circumstances, limits prohibitions to what seem reasonable, just, and consistent with the good news of Jesus Christ and the added new reality that non-Jews were becoming members of the Christian community. We change things today for the same reasons, because our experience teaches us to do so. The Old Testament itself set aside previous laws, and the New Testament does the same. Christians today can operate with the same premise in light of what we know within our experience, while still being faithful to the Gospel.

II Peter 2:4-8 and Jude 6-7—Some obscure examples— Additional passages often cited against homosexual acts are found in the New Testament in II Peter 2:4-8 and Jude vv. 6-7. Both are obscure passages, and one copies from the other. II Peter makes reference to a story that "God did not spare the angels when they sinned, but cast them into hell and committed them to chains of deepest darkness to be kept until the day of judgment" (II Peter 2:4 NRSV). The text continues in verse 2:6 by saying that Lot was "a righteous man greatly distressed by the licentiousness of the lawless" (2:7 NRSV). Jude parallels II Peter 2:4 by saying, "And the angels who did not keep their position, but left their proper dwelling, he has kept in eternal chains in deepest darkness for the judgment of the great Day" (Jude 6 NRSV). This immediately is followed by a reference to the sin of Sodom: "Likewise, Sodom and Gomorrah and the surrounding cities, which, in the same manner as they, indulged in sexual immorality, and pursued unnatural lust serve as an example by undergoing a punishment of fire" (Jude v. 7 NRSV). Thus the passages, though obscure, have been perceived by some as pejorative against homosexual acts.

To offer some clarity to these passages, some Jewish sources have seen the sin of Sodom as a desire to have sexual relations with *angels* (esp. *The Testament of Naphtali* 3:4-5). Other sources trace the reference to the Watchmen, or angelic creatures, who had intercourse with human women (Jubilees 7:21, quoting I Enoch). In this citation the sin of the angelic creatures is linked with Sodom's sin. These passages, in turn, refer to Genesis 6:1-4, in which the sons of God (which may refer to angels) had intercourse with the daughters of men, and there were giants in the earth. The Book of Jubilees says that this story refers to Sodom, where *angels and women* had intercourse. At best, it is a stretch of the imagination to cite the Jude and Second Peter passages as proof against homosexual acts. One can only wonder exactly what they prove at all.

I Corinthians 5:10-11 and 6:9—A laundry list of "sins"—In the midst of Paul's discussion of Christian freedom in I Corinthians 5-6, he twice presents lists of vices (I Cor. 5:10-11 and 6:9-10). Such cataloging of vices is a typical Hellenistic Jewish form of decrying the flagrant sins of pagans. These lists neither differentiate between grades of sinfulness,—idolatry and drunkenness are listed together,—nor does Paul differentiate between drunkenness and alcoholism, which we today classify as a treatable sickness. And the sins of the greedy are seen as no different from that of prostitutes and sodomites.

> Do you not know that wrongdoers will not inherit the kingdom of God? Do not be deceived! Fornicators, idolaters, adulterers, male prostitutes, sodomites, thieves, the greedy, drunkards, revilers, robbers—none of these will inherit the kingdom of God. (I Cor. 6:9-11 NRSV)

Paul sees any sexual immorality as a sign of the world's sinfulness, which stands under divine judgment. Justified believers are to leave such activities behind.

The second list in I Cor. 6:9-10 is of particular interest to the subject at hand, because it includes the terms *malakoi* and *arsenokoitai*. Careful word studies have shown that the I Corinthians and I Timothy references use terminology that suggests condemnation of pederasty, the sexual abuse of the young by adults, and the trafficking in children for sexual purposes. A common assumption by scholars is that *malakos* (singular) and *arsenokoites* (singular) referred to partners in a pederastic relationship, the *malakos* as passive and the *arsenokoites* as the active partner. Almost all English translations see these words as describing persons involved in homosexual activity. There is sufficient differentiation in the translations, however, that it indicates the ambiguity of their original meanings. Whatever their precise meanings may be, the words refer to exploitative practices between an adult and a child or young teen.

I Timothy 1:8-10—Rules for the "lawless"—In the I Timothy 1:8-10 text, once again we see ambiguities in interpretation regarding what Paul considers "lawless" activities.

> Now we know that the law is good, if one uses it legitimately. This means understanding that the law is laid down not for the innocent but for the lawless and disobedient, for the godless and sinful, for the unholy and profane, for those who kill their father or mother, for murderers, fornicators, sodomites, slave traders, liars, perjurers, and whatever else is contrary to sound teaching." (I Tim. 1:8-10 NRSV)

The writer is concerned that Christians must understand the proper use of the law. The function of the law is not for the righteous, but the lawless. The author then lists a catalogue of who the lawless are, including liars and perjurers, once again with no gradation in terms of their relative sinfulness. Again, as in the I Corinthians list, *arsenokoitai* appears. Some scholars see a significant pattern in the three successive words *pornois* (fornicators), *arsenokoitai* (translated as sodomites), and *andrapodistais* (slave traders). This may refer to the male who desires pederasty, and the slave trader who kidnaps or entraps the boy for pederastic prostitution. The point is that the meanings are too vague to make specific application to our modern understanding of homosexuality. The words, however, do imply the exploitation of persons rather than a consensual relationship.

Romans 1:18-32—Right with God; not law but grace—This is the passage of the New Testament that is quoted most often as reflecting God's judgment against homosexuality. It should be stated to begin with, however, that this passage can't be properly interpreted without a basic understanding of its social context. In much of the Greco-Roman world, pederasty, that is, same sex intercourse between and adult and a child or young teen, was extremely common, although, obviously, homosexual relations also occurred between consenting adults. This reality may have been significant in influencing Paul's aversion to homosexuality. It will not play a prominent role in our explanation, but it should be kept in mind.

Although we are not reprinting this rather lengthy passage from Romans, readers may wish to refer to the entire passage in conjunction with the following discussion of it. The point of the passage must be seen in the context of the whole scheme of the book of Romans. Paul's argument is that we are not made right with God by obedience to the law, in which we all fail miserably. Our righteousness comes from God's grace alone given to us in Jesus Christ.

Paul begins his argument in Romans 1 by condemning the gentiles for their idolatry. He argues that when we forsake the true God for idols, our whole life becomes idolatrous. Whatever it is that rules our lives, this is our god. When people worship created things rather than the Creator,—and when their passions dominate them,—these idolatries stand under the judgment of God. Therefore, God has abandoned them to their own devices. Paul calls this "the wrath of God." Their lives have become dominated by uncontrolled lust, debased sexual conduct, and other sinful behavior.

Paul says that women and men gave up intercourse with each other, "changing" their sexual behaviors "contrary to nature," being driven by a consuming passion to same-sex activity. Paul, thus, is condemning those whom he perceives as *heterosexuals* who are committing homosexual acts. They have thus rejected their *natural* inclination to monotheism and their *natural* inclination to the opposite sex. This, Paul says, is "against nature." It must be understood that the modern understanding of homosexuality as a constitutional condition was simply not a part of the ancient biblical understanding. It was assumed that everyone was basically heterosexual, and that to perform homosexual acts was contrary to one's own basic nature. It must be noted, however, that Paul's condemnation does not speak to the issue under discussion in the church and society today—which is the issue of adults, who are homosexual by nature, living in a non-exploitative, loving, monogamous faithful relationship.

Paul continues the passage with a whole catalogue of misconduct that flows from idolatry, some of which makes one wince because the shoe fits too closely. As Paul lists these unsavory examples of misconduct, who among us is not guilty of envy, slander, strife, deceit, gossiping, rebelliousness toward parents, and many of the other sins that he mentions? One wonders why it is that homosexuality is singled out by fundamentalistic conservatives as an abomination, when Paul mentions it as one of many sins that place us under the wrath of God. Paul continues his arguments by stressing that *all* of us are under the judgment of God, including those who stand in judgment against all of this gross conduct.

Paul's argument culminates at the beginning of Romans 2, where he says that when we self-righteously stand in judgment against others, we are appropriating the role of God as judge. In a surprising turn of events, he turns the judgmentalism of otherwise good people back upon themselves. *When we self-righteously stand in judgment against others, we are usurping that right which belongs to God alone.* This makes his pious audience idolaters as well. He traps them in their own "righteousness." Although he begins with a condemnation of the homosexual practices of his day to stir up the moral indignation of his readers, Paul uses this rhetorical mechanism to turn his criticism against his readers, and to us who make such judgments today. We are playing God. "All have sinned and come short of the glory of God," Paul declares, and "the wages of sin is death."

And what does Jesus say?

The Old and New Testament passages cited above are the sum total of the biblical passages that supposedly speak to the issue of homosexuality. Few realize that most of the passages are highly ambiguous, and several don't refer to homosexual practice at all. What is more, even fewer understand that the two main passages,— the story of the sin of Sodom, and Paul's diatribe in Romans 1, place the condemners themselves under condemnation. In the first instance, the Sodom story condemns our inhospitality, and in the Romans text, Paul places our judgmentalism, along side of homosexual acts, as being under the wrath of God!

Well then, does Jesus have anything to say on the subject of homosexual practice? Jesus' sayings on sexual mores are extremely few, particularly when compared with his words of condemnation on wealth and oppression. *There are no sayings of Jesus that bear any relation to homosexuality.* Even though arguments from silence are never conclusive, still, one might think that there would be at least one saying that Jesus addressed to what so many consider such a heinous sin.

The only sexual issues of importance to Jesus appear to have been monogamy, fidelity, and life-long commitment. (Compare Mark 10:2-9; Matthew 19:3-9.) He clearly thought sexuality should be expressed within a permanent and monogamous relationship. Thus, we believe that there is no inherent reason why unions between committed persons of the same sex could not have met Jesus' moral criteria.

Why is science important on this issue?

Among Christians the heart of the controversy over homosexuality involves not only the difference in how biblical interpretation is done, but also the appropriate role of science and other disciplines in shaping our worldview. It is appropriate, therefore, to mention briefly current scientific thinking related to homosexuality. Just as the early Christian church reevaluated Old Testament teachings in light of their contemporary situations, so also we today must refine our beliefs and thinking based on the input of reliable scientific research.

People who are judgmental about homosexuality simply want to believe that it is "perverted," living in defiance of a basic heterosexual nature, as Paul assumed. But scientific research in the past number of years gives dramatic support to the idea that sexual orientation is shaped by innate factors and that one is homosexual "by nature." There has been a decisive shift in understanding of the nature of homosexuality over the past four decades. Since 1973, the American Psychiatric Association has removed homosexuality from the category of mental illness to be treated. Now it is seen as a variable in the human sexual scheme of things.

The majority of psychiatrists and psychologists now agree that being gay or lesbian is no more of a choice than being heterosexual. Psychologists and counselors, from the experience of countless interviews, tell us that even when people wish *not* to be same-sex oriented, they cannot change the same-sex nature of their sexual fantasies. Social and biological scientific studies give increasing credence to the conclusion that homosexuality may be established before birth or in the very early formative years. Many specialists suspect homosexual orientation may be related to prenatal hormones; however, the causes of homosexuality and heterosexuality are not yet fully known.

It is a matter of heated controversy whether sexual orientation, once fixed, can be changed. The decision to change one's sexual orientation and the "treatment" undergone often doesn't have lasting effects. The American Psychiatric Association's position, as well as that of other professional groups, is that conversion therapy to change a person from a homosexual to a heterosexual orientation is not an appropriate method of treatment and frequently causes damage. Various interpretations are possible on this issue, but a growing body of scientific information suggests that homosexual orientation, at least for many, is a fixed reality that must be seriously studied.

The human side of the issue

Although homosexuality can be discussed Biblically and scientifically in a theoretical and dispassionate manner, as people of faith we know that at the heart of the issue we are talking about warm and vulnerable children of God. Counseling experience with homosexuals teaches us that the term "gay" is often a misnomer. Until gays and lesbians have worked through the process of affirming their own sexual identity, there can often be great personal struggle. Some experts feel that as many as 30% of teenage suicide attempts are due to homosexual anguish while coming to grips with their sexual orientation. Many of us know and love family, friends, and people in our faith community who are gay or lesbian. This experience takes the matter out of the realm of the theoretical. We are dealing with real, sensitive, often hurting, and loving people. Many homosexuals are persons of deep piety who want to share in the faith community. Some people reject family members when they "come out." Other family members, moved by faith and humanity, embrace them, sometimes with grieved bewilderment, but often with understanding and acceptance. In the process of "coming out" to the family, there are usually tears and a good deal of hugging and mutual expressions of love and concern. That family member is the same dear and wonderful person he or she has always been, but now the family understands his or her humanity and vulnerability with greater depth and perception.

Those who condemn may make harsh value judgments, but in doing so they are often not relating to human beings as they are. Human experience takes this whole issue of same-sex orientation out of the realm of the clinical and abstract. All of the old pejorative judgments sound unacceptable and inhumane when we are dealing with the beloved "bone of our bone and flesh of our flesh." If this is the liberal "homosexual agenda," then so be it. Is not this the nature of loving humanity? And is this not in the spirit of Jesus, who championed women and children? Who stood in solidarity with those whom others despised and deemed as outcasts? And who condemned the self-righteous and the oppressors?

A summary: looking through the lens of the gospel, science, and human experience

Ultimately, those of us who are Christians must struggle through the issue of homosexuality in light of the Gospel of the One who welcomed the outcast and the alien and who became an outcast and alien for us. It is this good news that can save us—heterosexual and homosexual alike—because the judgment of the law is just a prelude in Romans to the gospel that "all have been justified freely by his grace." Christians must distinguish in Scripture between the theological kernel of the good news in Jesus Christ and the cultural husk of the letter of the law. The same Scripture that seems to denounce homosexuality also seems to endorse slavery, rule out divorce, affirm the subordination of women, and call for obedience to any government, even though it is corrupt or tyrannical. How can we today embrace the denunciation of homosexuality and accept or overlook the others?

If Christ is the key to the Scripture, this gives us the freedom—even the obligation—to separate the theological kernel from the legal and cultural husk. The gospel interpretation frees us from the necessity of being fundamentalists or replicating the world picture of ancient history. Christians agree that being made right with God by grace,—the unearned love of God,—through faith in Jesus Christ is not only our answer for being at peace with God, but it is also the key to our scriptural interpretation.

Additionally, mainstream and truly evangelical churches must be open to the disciplines of learning as we address the issue of homosexuality, as well as other pressing issues of our time. If—as scientists are concluding more and more—sexual orientation is shaped by innate physiological and psychological processes, then are we talking about perversion or sin when we speak of the homosexual state of being? Are we not talking about how God creates human beings?

St. Augustine said that if Scripture seems to conflict with clear and certain reasoning, then we must reinterpret Scripture. We have done such reinterpretation regarding the heliocentric theory (which established that the earth is not the center of the universe, but it rotates around the sun); that we aren't living in a three storied universe with hell below and heaven above; that the world is infinitely older than we had previously thought; and that we must face the realities of evolution and relativity. We have reinterpreted Scripture by embracing the emancipation of slaves, and hopefully we are learning to accept the emancipation women, those divorced, and many other issues of changed understanding. If the sciences establish something that seems contrary to a clear text of Scripture, then, insofar as these scientific insights do not deny the gospel, we must see the text of Scripture in light of the new scientific data.

Let the healing begin

In conclusion, we are not suggesting that we close our eyes to sexual libertinism, whether that be heterosexual or homosexual. Some forms of homosexuality—and heterosexuality—including pederasty, are pathological and need to be treated as a deep-seated sickness. Homosexual orientation, however, need not be exploitative of others, or take dehumanizing forms, which were so evident in Paul's time, and in our own. Cannot people in a loving, self-giving same-sex relationship be reflective of God's new creation? Scripture tells us that it is not good for man—or woman— to be alone. Did not God make us for personal and communal relationships?

An informative editorial appeared in the *New York Times* published on September 17, 2005, which speaks to this issue. It points out that in 2003 the Massachusetts Supreme Court ruled that same-sex couples have the right to marry. The legislature then moved to overrule the decision by approving an amendment to ban gay marriages, but to approve of civil unions. When the same measure came before the legislature again, because a second vote was required on this amendment, it was defeated by a margin of 157 to 39! The main reason for this about-face is that over 6,600 same-sex couples were married over the course of the year without any sign of adverse effects. As the editorial states, "The sanctity of heterosexual marriages has not been destroyed. Public morals have not gone into a tailspin . . . Gay marriage, it turned out, is good for family values."

Ever mindful of human frailty and the need for forgiveness—first of all, for ourselves—are we being called to lift up the ideal of monogamous, covenantal, and life-long relationships, no matter what one's sexual orientation? Is not this the alternative to both heterosexual and homosexual promiscuity? And should not the church recognize the blessing of God on the estate of two persons living together in a same-sex relationship by giving them good counsel and consecrating their relationship with the blessings of pastors and the whole church?

If, as Scripture says, Christ has broken down the dividing wall between people, then for Christ's sake, for the sake of our sisters and brothers of same-sex orientation, and for our own sake, let us be truly Christian—and truly inclusive. "There is no longer Jew or Greek, there is no longer slave or free, there is no longer male or female." Dare we say there is no longer heterosexual and homosexual? "For all of you are one in Christ Jesus." (Galatians 3:28 NRSV)

Some final thoughts

Members of the religious right claim that same-sex marriage is destroying family values. Campaigns are being launched on both federal and state levels to pass constitutional amendments to ban same-sex marriage. Apart from whipping up emotions among people to vote for right wing causes and candidates, this hate and fear mongering has nothing at all to do with protecting family values. These actions are in the same category as anti-miscegenation laws which banned interracial marriages. In both cases, such laws are discriminatory and ultimately unconstitutional. If such witch hunting is to be carried to its logical conclusions in the name of family values, then why not a constitutional amendment to ban divorce? Interestingly enough, statistics show that the percentage of divorces among evangelicals is higher than in the general population (*"Christians are more likely to experience divorce than are non-Christians,"* Barna Research Group, 1999-DEC-21, at: *http://www.barna.org/cgi-bin/*). Why not also push for a constitutional ban against couples living together outside of marriage, which statistically is higher than those who cohabit within marriage? How can same-sex marriage be destructive of family values when such a marriage discourages promiscuity and is a commitment of two people to live together in a life-long covenantal relationship of monogamy and fidelity? Think about it!

Making a difference

Since this is one of the great divisive issues of our time, and because we affirm that Christ has broken down the dividing wall among people, here are some reconciling suggestions that can encourage civil debate on the issue.

- Remind people that the Bible does not speak of homosexuality as we now understand and use the term and that the Judeo-Christian Scriptures do not condemn homosexuals—or heterosexuals—living together in loving, monogamous, and covenantal relationships.
- If your state is contemplating an amendment banning gay marriage, remind those who always want to make this a biblical issue of what the Bible really says or does not say related to homosexuality.
- Emphasize the fact that liberals are indeed pro-family and that being pro-family doesn't equate with being against gay marriage.
- Keep informed about evolving scientific information about the nature and causes of homosexuality.
- Advocate for equal treatment of gays and lesbians.

- Be supportive of gays and lesbians who have been rejected by their families and their communities.
- Work to ensure that your place of worship is open and welcoming to all people.

Talking Points

- **Our Approach to the Biblical Text Involves Dialogue with Science and Human Experience.**

  Because most of the outrage about issues of homosexuality comes from fundamentalist Christians, this chapter deals with the issues in Christian categories. This requires dialogue between biblical texts, the sciences, and our human experiences.

- **There Is an Element of Change within Scripture Itself.**

  Scripture does not speak with a single voice. As time passed, one command was overruled by another. "Christian anthropology" uses ancient texts to subjugate people, including homosexuals. This approach reduces the divine will to absolute demands, refusing to recognize that God's movement in history changes the nature of things.

- **Old Testament Passages Cited against Homosexuality Are Not All Applicable.**

  An overview of the Old Testament passages referring to homosexual activity shows that some are mistranslations due to preconceived notions. Others are enmeshed among commands which obviously no longer apply. The Old Testament passage most often quoted (Genesis 19) to attack homosexual activity is in reality talking about gang rape as an attack on basic civility and hospitality.

- **New Testament Passages Also Must be Examined in Their Contexts.**

  Some of the quoted New Testament passages are ambiguous. Analysis of other passages shows they may refer to pederasty (adults exploiting children) among other factors. The most important New Testament passage, Romans 1, is treated in depth to show that Paul puts *all people* under God's judgment so that *all* might share in the grace of God in Jesus Christ. In the four Gospels, Jesus affirms monogamy and fidelity, but says nothing about homosexuality.

- **Dialogue with the Sciences Informs Us about the Nature of Homosexuality**

  Scientific research gives support to the idea that sexual orientation is shaped by innate factors and that a person is homosexual "by nature." Since 1973, the American Psychiatric Association no longer sees homosexuality as a treatable condition, but as a variable in the human sexual scheme of things.

- **A Compassionate Approach to the Gay and Lesbian Experience Is More Than Theoretical.**

  When we relate with gays and lesbians in our personal relationships, the whole issue is taken out of the realm of the theoretical. We are dealing with real, often hurting, sensitive, and loving people. Motivated by love expressed in Jesus, we can be Christ to others and see Christ in others.

6

Haves and Have-nots:
THAT'S A Family Values Issue!

A number of years ago we heard a sermon in which the preacher said, "My first point is that 34 million [at that time] people live in poverty in the United States. My second point is that far too many people don't give a damn about it. And my third point is that you who are listening to me are probably more upset about the fact that I said 'damn' in my sermon than you are about those who are suffering from poverty." A nation that ignores its poor or places stumbling blocks in the way of success, whose supreme god is money, is a nation that walks in the opposite direction of its God. This chapter focuses on the causes and realities of poverty in the United States and advocates some effective responses.

As this is being written, 37 million people—12.7 percent of the United States population—live in poverty in what is the richest country in the world. This represents an increase of 1.1 million persons since 2003 and a 17 percent increase since 2000. Yet, in recent years, especially since the advent of welfare reform, poverty has become almost a non-issue for Democrats and Republicans alike. In the aftermath of Hurricane Katrina, poverty once again was thrust into the American consciousness—and hopefully the American conscience as well—as we expressed shock and dismay at the images of people too poor or weak to escape. They'd been there all along; it's just that they were unnoticed. Now that our country has been reminded of their presence, there are really only two choices: to either continue looking the other way, or to make this a teachable moment and act accordingly. It is our hope that this chapter will enhance our collective understanding of wealth and poverty issues so that the shame of poverty in our own country can be more effectively confronted.

OK, So I'm rich. Is that immoral?

While this chapter will focus primarily on poverty, it's difficult to talk about poverty without acknowledging that, in this country at least, it occurs in the midst of great wealth. Lest it appear that we are about to begin a diatribe against wealth, we want to state upfront that wealth is not necessarily a bad thing. It can be a blessing if it is used judiciously, viewed as a gift to be shared, and not acquired at the expense of others. We are told in Genesis 13:2 that Abraham had great wealth. Job was twice blessed with substantial material possessions. There are several passages in the Old Testament (for example, Deuteronomy 8: 28, Proverbs 22:2, Ecclesiastes 5:19) in which wealth is seen as evidence of God's blessing. At the same time, Genesis (1:26-30; 5:18) also reminds us that in reality all that we have belongs to God. The psalmist (Psalms 24:1) tells us that "The earth is the Lord's and everything in it." God gifts this all to us, or perhaps loans it to us would be more accurate, and thus, we are to be good stewards of what we receive. Jesus, in the Parable of the Talents (Matthew 25:14-30), makes it clear that what we are given we are to use wisely. If we don't, it can lead to God's judgment, as happened to the rich man who constantly ignored the beggar Lazarus (Luke 16:19-31).

Although the Bible affirms the fact that wealth can be a blessing, it also places some significant restrictions on the acquisition and use of wealth. Believers are cautioned not to put their ultimate trust in wealth, but in God (Proverbs 11:4, 28; Jeremiah 9:23; 1 Timothy 6:17; James 1:11, 5:2). That's basically what the First Commandment is all about: "You shall have no other gods." Martin Luther, the father of the Protestant Reformation, said (Large Catechism, First Commandment) "Your God is that in which you place your love and your trust." Or as the more contemporary theologian, Paul Tillich put it, whatever is your "ultimate concern" is your god. Whenever wealth becomes our ultimate concern, we have set up a false god to worship.

What's more, consistently throughout the Scriptures, it is made clear that God wants us to be most careful of the means that we use to acquire our wealth. When wealthy people in the Bible were condemned, it was often because of the unjust ways in which they became wealthy. Amos (4:11, 5:11) spoke passionately against the injustice of obtaining wealth through oppression or fraud. Micah (6:1) was eloquent in his condemnation of the use of unjust scales and light weights with which Israel defrauded the poor. Throughout history, and certainly continuing into the present day, there are similar examples of situations in which wealth has been acquired at the expense of others. Slavery, child labor, starvation wages, corrupt governments and corporations, racism and sexism all have been part of a systemic effort to accrue wealth through the oppression and abuse of other people. Wealth accumulated in this way is not a blessing from God; it is an abuse of what in reality belongs to God.

Perhaps one of the most difficult questions that people of faith grapple with is how much financial wealth is sufficient. Or, on the other hand, what constitutes insufficient financial resources? Again, the Scriptures can be informative. Proverbs 30:8 says, "Give me neither poverty nor riches . . . . Otherwise I may have too much and disown you and say 'Who is the Lord?' Or I may become poor and steal, and so dishonor the name of God." Saint Paul, in I Timothy 6:6 tells us that "if we have food and clothing we will be content."

How does this relate to our situation today? What we know is that the gap between rich and poor in this country continues to widen. According to the federal government, the poverty line for a family of four is roughly $19,200 per year. At the other end of the spectrum, the Survey of Consumer Finances, sponsored by the Federal Reserve Board, suggests that wealth is becoming concentrated in the hands of a few people. The wealthiest one percent of households owns roughly 33.4 percent of the nation's net worth; the top ten percent of households own over 71 percent; and the bottom 40 percent of households own less than one percent of the net worth. So, no matter how you "slice the pie," this seems an unfair and unjust set of circumstances. If we believe that every person is created in the image of God, must we not also be about the business of ensuring that the resources God has given us are used to promote the wellbeing of all?

Poverty is immoral

Poverty is of course a social and economic issue, but for people of faith it is first and foremost a moral issue. In other words, it should be addressed from the standpoint of how it relates to common standards of goodness and decency. There are over 300 verses in the Christian Scriptures that speak about poverty and injustice, as compared with hardly a handful that even conceivably address abortion or homosexuality. We could say to our friends on the religious right who insist on using abortion or homosexuality as the single-issue litmus test on morality that, based on the Bible, the key moral issue that should be addressed is how we can serve the poor. The Old Testament prophets constantly advocated for the care of the poor, promoting the "shalom" life, in other words a life of wholeness, in which people can be and become everything that God wills for them. In ancient Israel there were laws that periodically released people from long-term poverty, that forgave their debts, and returned them to their rightful status in the community (Leviticus 25, Deuteronomy 15).

Early Christians organized their lives around the elimination of poverty barriers. Acts 2 tells us that "they would sell their possessions and goods and distribute the proceeds to all, as any had need." Throughout the Gospels Jesus showed his compassion for the poor and his impatience with those who oppressed people living in poverty. He said, "I have come that they might have life and that they might have it abundantly" (John 10:10) and "You shall love your neighbor as yourself" (Matthew 19:19b).

Jesus didn't just *talk* about poverty, however; he *was* one of the poor himself. Far too often we hear well-meaning people dismissing concern for poverty by quoting Jesus' statement in Mark 14:7, that "The poor shall always be with us." But they miss the point. Jesus wasn't condoning constant poverty. Instead, he was saying, "The poor will be around whenever you decide to minister to them. I will not be with you physically forever, but my ministry must continue through you. And you must look for me in the hungry and the oppressed. Their face is my face. What you do to them, you do to me."

When we look at the faces of poverty in this country, do we see Jesus? More than 13 million children have inadequate food to eat. Nearly 80 percent of those living in poverty are women and children. Over 45 million people are without health insurance. These are not just statistics; they represent real people. They are our neighbors. In spite of this, it sometimes seems that much of American society, and certainly much of our leadership, has lost its moral compass when it comes to doing something significant about reducing poverty. Concerns about private morality seem to take precedence over the social welfare of 37 million of our own citizens who live in poverty. Private morality is a noble trait; however, when we knowingly allow children to go to bed hungry; when we watch people die from lack of medical care; when we amass personal fortunes at the expense of others, we are deviating from what is commonly considered right or proper or good. That's immorality, both private and public. It is immoral, and certainly not in the best interest of the future strength of our country to allow a sizable part of the next generation to be inadequately housed, fed, educated, or trained to earn a sustainable adequate income. This is not a legacy we dare to leave for our children and grandchildren.

Pope John Paul II, inspired by the parable of the rich man and poor Lazarus, said this in his homily at Yankee Stadium in 1979: "We cannot stand idly by, enjoying our own riches and freedom if, in any place, the Lazarus of the 20th century stands at our doors . . . . The rich man and Lazarus are both human beings, both of them equally created in the image and likeness of God, both of them equally redeemed by Christ." As people of good will, as people of faith, it is clear that we are compelled to respond.

The poverty trap

When people fall into poverty, numerous barriers keep them there. Contrary to what many people believe, laziness or personal failure, although they may on occasion be contributing factors, are not the major causes of poverty. Most people living in poverty are neither unambitious, lacking in intelligence, nor "good-for-nothing." Some are born into situations of "generational poverty" where they sometimes have few options for getting out of it or don't know how to access the proper resources for doing so. Many others have had the misfortune to fall into "situational poverty" in which their lack of resources are due to particular sets of events or circumstances. Most people struggling against poverty are just regular, decent people who try to "play by the rules" and are committed to American values. In fact, nearly 40 percent of those living in poverty are employed, unfortunately at jobs that do not pay a livable wage.

There are many reasons why people fall into poverty. It could be the loss of a family farm, geographic isolation—as for example the concentration of poor families in ghettos—substandard educations, downsizing of jobs, lack of job opportunities, death of a spouse, accidents, natural disasters, divorce, crop losses, illnesses, or lack of health insurance, or any one of numerous other situations that can throw people into an impoverished lifestyle. If poverty is to be addressed effectively it is important to recognize first of all some of the barriers that can make it difficult for people to climb out of poverty. In reality these roadblocks often represent actions that the non-poor take to avoid dealing with the issue.

Isolation from the poor—Perhaps one of the greatest barriers is that people of privilege too often remain geographically, physically, and emotionally far removed from people in poverty.

We write our checks, pack Christmas and Easter baskets, donate our cast-off clothing to salve our consciences, but rarely do we come face to face with the poor. Poverty remains hidden, and because we are separated from each other, we fall victim to our myths about each other, and our responses remain inadequate, if not downright insulting. When this barrier is broken, we discover that it can change our lives. We begin to see—really see—the faces and the lives of the poor, and we either have to conclude that we really don't care, or we have to become involved in very personal ways.

Poverty as an individual, not a social problem—We've all heard the excuses. *"They* shouldn't have so many babies . . . *They* are lazy . . . *Everyone* can make it if they try." When poverty is seen as a personal failure or as evidence of some sort of inherent weakness on the part of those who are poor, it becomes much easier to absolve ourselves from any responsibility, or at best, to only respond with immediate charity relief. When that happens, policies and practices that perpetuate poverty—as for example low wages, poor health care, substandard living conditions, and inadequate educational opportunities—are not addressed, and significant meaningful change doesn't occur.

Women are valued less than men—Sexism continues to play a role in the lives of low-income women. Women and children comprise nearly 80 percent of the poverty population. High-paying manufacturing jobs have given way to lower-paying jobs in the service sector. Women are often relegated to the lowest paid positions in service-oriented jobs with minimal or no benefits. Child care options are limited. When children are sick and mom must be absent, women are seen as less dependable. In 2004 women's earnings decreased by one percent, and women earned only 77 cents for every dollar earned by men. There still is the assumption that women don't need as much because their spouse or someone else will help support them.

Racism as a factor—There is a racist legacy of unequal access in this country, and even though laws have made such discrimination illegal it still exists and has a disproportionate impact on people of color. African Americans and Hispanics account for over half of the homeless population in the United States. Neonatal deaths among blacks are 14.5 per thousand in contrast to 6.3 deaths per thousand among whites. While racism may not be as overt as in the past, even more insidiously, it often takes the form of benign neglect. This is particularly destructive for the next generation of people of color. For example, Marian Wright Edelman of the Children's Defense Fund points out that race continues to be the defining factor in many American schools. She notes that as a result of policy changes over the last decade, American schools are actually resegregating, with almost three-quarters of Black and Latino students attending predominantly minority schools.

Inadequate economic support structures—When one looks at some of the existing economic roadblocks within our society it is easier to understand why low-income people might feel as though they were shoveling sand against the tide. The minimum hourly wage of $5.15 hasn't been raised since 1997, even though in 2004 the official U.S. poverty level of $19,200 for a family of four would require a minimum wage of $8.70. When inflation is factored in, the buying power of the minimum wage has shrunk even lower. With the shift in this country from a manufacturing and industrial job base to a service-oriented base, high paying jobs have become less accessible to many. Thus, even though employment rates may go down, increasingly more people have been forced to take low-wage jobs, often with few or no benefits.

Other factors compound the situation. Low wages coupled with the inflated housing market during the past decade or so has put safe and affordable housing beyond the reach of many. According to figures provided by the U.S. Department of Health and Human Services, up to 600,000 men, women, and children go homeless each night in the U.S. The Coalition on Human Needs notes that in 2003, approximately 5.3 million households in the U.S. were paying at least half of their yearly earnings on housing, leaving little extra for other essentials. And if they are among the over 45 million people who are living without health insurance, it's no wonder that one catastrophic illness would push them even deeper into the poverty pit.

Lack of political muscle—Finally, one result of the lack of material goods is a corresponding lack of political power. People who are struggling to survive from day to day don't have the resources to make campaign contributions or, often, even the time to become involved in community or political organizations. In the midst of situations such as this, the real tragedy is that our current elected leaders seem to place a priority on providing tax cuts and other benefits for the wealthy—a welfare program for the rich—by cutting basic human services programs that benefit the poor. Under those circumstances it can be difficult to feel that it is possible to make a difference through voting or other actions. Unfortunately, the voices of the poor remain muted and poverty far too often remains hidden.

Striving for justice

The nature of the human dilemma in history is one of suffering and injustice. Yet, God's intent, as reflected in Matthew 25 and elsewhere, is that we be delivered from this dilemma. We know the command, but it is often difficult to implement. An old newspaper clipping, that is a parody on the words of Matthew 25, is instructive:

I was hungry and you formed a committee and discussed my hunger.

I was imprisoned and you crept off quietly and prayed for my release.

I was naked and in your mind you debated the morality of my appearance.

I was sick and you thanked God for your health.

I was homeless and you preached to me of the spiritual shelter of the love of God.

I was lonely and you left me alone to pray for me.

You seem so holy; so very close to God. But I'm still very hungry, and lonely, and cold.

Dr. Martin Luther King understood this when he said, "We are called to play the Good Samaritan on life's roadside. But that will only be an initial act. One day the whole Jericho Road must be transformed so that men and women will not be beaten or robbed as they make their journey through life." Within the context of poverty, this means undertaking actions that not only offer emergency assistance but also keep people out of poverty, restore their dignity, and empower them to become productive members of society. In other words, we seek justice, the standard by which the benefits and penalties of living in society are distributed. Justice seeks wholeness in individuals and society. We believe that three approaches, used in combination, and ranging from the individual to the collective, offer a wholistic and just approach to poverty.

Charity—In this country we have a long and noble history of responding to immediate emergency needs. Churches and other charitable institutions have recognized that when people are hungry they need to be fed. When they are cold they must be clothed, and when they are homeless they must be brought in out of the cold. Americans once again showed their generosity in responding to the immediate needs of the tens of thousands left without food or shelter in the aftermath of Hurricanes Katrina and Rita. Ten days after the hurricane hit, donors had already given over $600 million for relief efforts.(*Christian Century,* October 4, 2005, p. 12). Surveys of charitable giving around the world show that America gives more money as a percentage of the gross domestic product than any country except Israel. (*The Chicago Tribune*, October 2, 2005, Section 2, page 1) Obviously, we cannot stop offering our help to those in need. It literally saves lives.

So, what is the downside to charity? Consider for a moment what happens to people if we always just "do for" them. It certainly runs the risk of perpetuating dependency; but even more distasteful is the fact that "doing for" always implies that we have positions of power over those we "help." We decide what they get and when they get it. Our giving makes us feel good while the poor remain with us. We give our excess to people we rarely or never see. Exercising our power or control in that way is inappropriate, especially for Christians who are committed to loving their neighbors as themselves.

Empowerment—Because charity constitutes only a beginning response to poverty, it is important to look at ways in which people can be supported as they work to overcome poverty situations—ways that contribute to self-sufficiency and empowerment. As one low-income woman shared with us recently, "What is empowering to me is discovering for myself what I can do about my situation." If that is the case, it makes sense to offer opportunities for people in poverty to achieve economic independence. Literacy training, tutoring, self-employment programs, classes in financial management, and voter registration drives in low-income communities are just a few examples of how people of good will can stand with those who are economically disadvantaged. Churches and other non-profit groups are often well-equipped to do this. As some would say, such activities offer a "hand-up, not a hand-out." And that is one philosophy shared by liberals and conservatives alike. However, although these actions of charity and empowerment are essential, they represent an incomplete response to poverty unless at the same time there is a concerted effort to address the societal root causes of poverty. As Dr. King said, "True compassion is more than flinging a coin at a beggar; it comes to see that an edifice which produces beggars needs restructuring."

Systemic change—The reality is that there are unjust systems and structures in our country and our world that maintain poverty and injustice. Systemic change—macrocosmic change—is necessary to confront some of the root causes of poverty. There is a need to address the reordering of our national priorities—globalization and its impact on poverty, health care, military spending, war, funding for education, to name a few. Remember, as the 2003 statement on poverty by the U.S. National Conference of Catholic Bishops pointed out, "The economy exists for the person, not the person for the economy." People should have priority over profits.

Working for systemic change means being involved in the political arena, something that far too many Christians have been reluctant to do. But Jesus was not afraid to confront the injustices in the society of his day, and neither should we. We know that in reality, *we* are the governors, and our elected officials are the governed. Conservatives understand this as well and have been masterful at making their views heard and felt. So if we really wish to be effective at combating poverty, we have the responsibility to use our gift of citizenship to promote the development of local, state, and national programs and policies that are in the best interest of the most vulnerable among us. As people who are called to be good stewards of God's creation, we pay taxes to the government so that it can, in our name, fulfill its responsibility to ensure that its constituents have access to a sufficient livelihood.

Because there seems to be a trend by at least some in government circles to encourage religious and private organizations to assume ever-broadening responsibility for the social welfare of our citizens, we must emphasize that in the "war" on poverty, governmental support is essential. Even if churches and other private organizations invested their maximum resources, that would not be enough to counteract the powerful forces that control our country and world. For example, when global interest rates rise by only a few percentage points, that increases the amount of foreign debt owed by poor nations already overburdened by poverty, effectively neutralizing the amount of relief and development aid that comes from churches and private organizations. Similarly, when our own legislators make cuts in governmental social service programs, it is extremely difficult for the religious and charitable effort to compensate. In fact, charitable giving to human service endeavors has declined every year, from a peak of $22.1 billion in 2001 to $19.2 billion in 2004 (*Christian Century*, October 4, 2005, p. 12). That amount is dwarfed by the billions of dollars in aid to America's poor that come from government programs.

Poverty is a family values issue

Conservatives love to talk about family values; yet, adequate governmental family support policies in this country are severely lacking. When as a country we truly value families, we will ensure that all families have the safety networks that will keep them from falling into poverty. Single mothers with children are the most economically vulnerable group in the United States, a critical situation that must be addressed by liberals and conservatives alike. The same is true in many European countries; however, because these countries tend to have universal family policies, most of those women don't sink into poverty. These universal family policies are not "welfare" programs as we have in the U.S. Instead, they provide services such as health care, day care, education, family allowances, and child support that are available to *all* families

When as a country we truly value families, we will ensure that all children, whatever their ethnic background or race, will have the opportunity to receive a solid educational foundation in non-segregated schools. Jonathan Kozol in his book *The Shame of the Nation: The Restoration of Apartheid Schooling in America* points out that all over the country, states spend less in school districts with high numbers of minority students than in districts with the fewest minority students.

When as a country we truly value families, we will work to reduce the increasing income disparity between rich and poor families. Our country has the most unequal income distribution and one of the highest poverty rates of all advanced world economies. The day after Hurricane Katrina hit land, the U.S. Census Bureau released its annual report, "Income, Poverty, and Health Insurance Coverage in the United States." An analysis of this report shows that although the portion of the total national income earned by the bottom 60 percent of families did not increase in the previous year, the portion going to the wealthiest five percent increased; and when we consider the average inflation-adjusted family income, these wealthiest families actually received a 1.7 percent increase in earnings.

When as a country we truly value families, we will not allow 45.8 million people to be denied health insurance. It is estimated that seventy percent of the uninsured are in families where at least one member is employed. For the last four years employer-sponsored health insurance coverage declined. According to the

Employee Benefit Research Institute, the percentage of individuals with employee-sponsored health insurance fell from 64 percent to 60 percent between 2000 and 2004. And nearly one quarter of people in households earning less than $25,000 are uninsured, while only eight percent of those with incomes of over $75,000 are without health insurance. In the long run, people who avoid seeing a doctor because they can't afford it can ultimately be an even more expensive drain on our health care system.

When as a country we truly value families, we will not let poverty destroy or maim any of our children: those who are born sick because their mothers never received prenatal care; those who were never immunized against childhood diseases; those left home alone because parents couldn't find quality affordable child care. Nicholas Kristof, in a September 6, 2005 article in the *New York Times*, points out that the infant mortality rate in the U.S. has risen for the first time since 1958, and our country now ranks 43rd in the world in terms of how many children die. Nationally 29 percent of children had no health insurance at some point in the last twelve months. In terms of immunizations, the U.S. ranks 84th for measles and 89th for polio. It is estimated that 50 of the 77 babies who die each day die because of poverty.

When as a country we truly value families, we will support efforts to ensure that all families have adequate shelter. According to statistics from the Evangelical Lutheran Church in America's Office on Governmental Affairs, there is a two million unit gap in available and affordable housing for the lowest income people and the number of people who need housing. A 2003 U.S. Conference of Mayors study of 25 cities found that in 84 percent of these cities, emergency shelters indicated that they have had to turn away homeless families due to lack of resources.

When as a country we truly value families, we will ensure that *all* children and families are a priority concern to us as individuals, to our churches and other social institutions, and to our elected officials at all levels of government. All it takes is our commitment to do something about it.

But, do we have the will to eliminate poverty?

Poverty can be addressed effectively if there is the moral and political will to do so. Why should we continue to have such a significant degree of poverty in this, the wealthiest country in the world? We, of all countries in the world, have the resources to do something about it. To place this in a global perspective, the 2005 report issued by the U.N. Development Program notes that a total of $7 billion dollars annually from wealthy countries could provide 2.6 billion people with clean drinking water and cost less than Europeans spend on perfume, or that Americans spend on cosmetic surgery(*New York Times*, September 13, 2005, "Meet the Fakers" by Nicholas Kristof). Obviously, inadequate resources are not the problem.

What has been missing, in our country and around the world, is the collective moral and political will, if not to eliminate, at least to significantly reduce poverty. Morally, we know that we are to love our neighbors as ourselves. Politically, we have it in our power to insist that our elected officials reorder our national priorities. In order for this to happen, however, it also means that we as individuals must be prepared to sacrifice and reduce our own dependence on material things in order that others can have more. That will be the true measure of our commitment.

Making a difference

One of the first steps in bringing hope and healing to people who live in poverty is to acknowledge that we can indeed make a difference. Here are some ways to begin.

- Become an informed citizen. Learn about those issues that have a direct impact on the lives of low-income families.
- Seek out interactions with persons living in poverty. Be open to their hospitality and to building relationships with them.
- Engage in open and honest debate and discussion, as liberals and conservatives, Republicans and Democrats in formulating ideas for what might be effective.

- Be intentional about not only offering charity, but also supporting programs that empower people living in poverty and joining with others in addressing the root causes of poverty in our society.
- Insist that our elected representatives stop supporting programs that favor the wealthy at the expense of everyone else. Support and vote for those candidates who are committed to giving the poor a fair shake.
- Publicly recognize the huge cost of the Iraq war and resources it has directed away from the poor and marginalized. Work for peace throughout the world so that more resources can be used to attack the causes of poverty
- Encourage our churches not only to issue pious statements and pronouncements but also to make sacrificial financial commitments to the poor.

Talking Points

- **Wealth, of itself, is not a bad thing.**

  Wealth, as the Bible points out, can be a blessing as long as it is recognized that everything we have ultimately belongs to God. Thus we should be good stewards of what we have received. Wealth should not be accumulated or maintained in ways that are unjust. In our country there is a huge disparity between the resources of the rich and those of the poor.
- **Poverty should be addressed as a moral issue.**

  We address the issue of poverty from the standpoint of how it relates to common standards of goodness and decency. The Old Testament prophets advocated for the poor, and early Christians organized their lives around elimination of poverty barriers. Today, concerns about individual, private morality seem to take precedence over the social welfare of the poor. Ignoring the needs of the economically vulnerable is immoral and not in the best interest of the future of our country.

- **When people fall into poverty, numerous barriers keep them there.**

  Most people living in poverty are decent people who are committed to American values. Among the barriers that keep people from climbing out of poverty are isolation, the perception that poverty is an individual rather than a social problem, the second-class status of women, racism, inadequate economic support structures, and lack of political muscle.

- **Poverty is a justice issue.**

  Addressing poverty means working for justice, the standard by which the benefits and penalties of living in society are distributed. Three approaches, used in combination, offer a just and wholistic approach to poverty: charity, empowerment, and systemic change. Religious and private organizations can't fight poverty alone. Governmental involvement is essential.

- **Poverty is a family values issue.**

  Universal family policies, rather than "welfare" programs should be available to all families, not just the poor. Such policies ensure that all people receive a solid educational foundation, a sustainable living wage, adequate health insurance, and adequate shelter.

- **Poverty can be addressed effectively if there is the moral and political will to do so.**

  The United States, of all countries in the world, has the necessary resources to combat poverty. Morally, we know that we should love our neighbors as ourselves, and politically we have the power to set national policies and priorities. We just need to do so.

7

Environmentalist, Conservationist, Tree Hugger, or Steward?

The world seemed to be a gentler place when "tree hugger" was about the most pejorative descriptor applied to those who expressed concern about the environment. In more recent years as nightmares about global warming, high fuel prices, ineffective fuel economy standards, and increasing destruction of the environment have come into public debate, the terms used to describe environmentalists have risen in decibel and toxicity too. Into this mix of the sometimes competing interests between preservationists and consumerists come the ideologies of the conservative religionists. That added ingredient is the primary subject of this chapter.

Arousing suspicions

Some fundamentalistic conservatives are deeply suspicious about environmentalists. Some believe that they should only worship God and not creation. Some believe that the end of the world and the return of Jesus are near, so worrying about ruining the environment is time wasted. Yet, the consistent record in the Old and New Testaments shares the story that God created (to bring order out of chaos) everything by pronouncing it into existence. The persons of the Triune God—Father, Son, and Holy Spirit—are each identified in the accounts of creation (Genesis 1, John 1) and the creative activities of God are assumed to be continuing.

In spite of the centrality of the scriptural doctrine of creation, historically there has been a lack of interest among Christians about the environment. In addition, it was Lynn White (White, Lynn, 1967, "The historical roots of our ecological crisis." *Science* 155, March 10, 1967, pp. 1203-1207.) who almost forty years ago strongly suggested that Christians shared much of the blame for the injury to the environment. For example, he said that Christianity is, "the most anthropocentric religion the world has seen," and it bears a "huge burden of guilt" for teaching attitudes about the environment that have brought us to the current state. He also suggests that "we shall continue to have a worsening ecologic crisis until we reject the Christian axiom that nature has no reason for existence save to serve man."

A misunderstanding

An initial point of departure for discussion on this matter lies in a misunderstanding. There is a misunderstanding of the biblical phrase that God gave "dominion" over the earth to humankind. The proper understanding of "dominion" is that humans are given use of the earth as a trust or as something we are borrowing. God has created and "owns" the earth. Humans are not entitled to exploit it or destroy it but simply to use it for human benefit as God intended. Almost a century ago, a pastor named Frank Buchman (http://en.thinkexist.com/quotes/frank_buchman/) said that "there is enough in the world for everyone's need, but not enough for everyone's greed." It is this short catchy phrase that seems to divide people generally and Christians specifically in terms of their perspectives on the use of the environment. Those who think in terms of "need" seek to maintain and improve a sustainable planet for the good of all. Those who think in terms of "greed" appear to think that the planet is to be used (and used up) to satisfy individual desires.

The Bible passage that has given rise to the "greedy" interpretation is Genesis 1:26 where it says, "Then God said, "Let us make man in our image, in our likeness, and let them rule over the fish of the sea and the birds of the air, over the livestock, over all the earth, and over all the creatures that move along the ground." (NIV). While much has been written about the meaning of "dominion", or "rule" in the version quoted, a best case can be made for the position that humankind has been given an obligation to care for all of creation.

As one reviews the first chapters of the Book of Genesis, several basic views about the natural world and the roles we play in it are developed. The beginning verses attest to the belief that God created all life and it all is good. In Genesis 2:7, adam, the word for "human being" or "earth creature," is formed "from the dust of the earth." The word adam is really a play on the word adamah which means "earth" or "ground." In short, the name of the original human demonstrates the strong connection between the earth and human beings. The same can be said about the well-known story of Noah. In preparing for the flood, Noah was instructed to gather a male and a female of every species, demonstrating God's promise of care "for every living thing."

Placing these concepts together, the first few chapters of the Hebrew Scriptures undergird the perspective that God created all life, defined it as good, made the first human from earthly soil, and showed caring concern for all creatures. As God respects the earth and values its many life forms, so also are we to do likewise.

We are not to dominate the earth, but rather to be stewards (caretakers) of the creation. The Psalmist (24:1) reminds us that the "earth is the Lord's and everything in it." Our calling is to manage and care for the earth as a God-given trust for which we will be held accountable. In our own understanding of the concept of a steward or manager, it is one who operates under authority that is given by another—authority that can be quite broad even though limited by the owner. A steward has the right to receive personal benefit from her stewardship, but not the right to own that from which benefit is derived. In short, a steward advances and preserves the interests of the owner to whom she is accountable.

So it is in our human existence relative to God. The dominion with which God has gifted us is unearned, unmerited, and freely given. The small planet which God has also given us is the place where we exercise that dominion, humbly and gratefully and in concert with the will of the Owner. As that Owner said to the first human with regard to stewardship of the environment, "till it and keep it" (Gen. 2:15).

So how did we get here?

There are surely historic and current Christian interpretations of "dominion" over the natural world that have supported environmental exploitation. Thomas Aquinas in his *Summa Contra Gentiles* (Notre Dame: University of Notre Dame Press, 1975), for example, said that non-intellectual creatures (any non-human creatures) are only to be valued in terms of their usefulness to humans. Thomas' perspective is very much like that of Origen who in his *Contra Celsum* (Cambridge: Cambridge University Press, 1953, IV, 78 and 74) argued that God made everything primarily for the use of humans. In both of these examples, however, their arguments are based on Greek and Stoic philosophies instead of the Christian Scriptures.

By the time of the Reformation, the influence of both Aquinas and Origen seemed to continue in the writings of both Luther and Calvin. In his comments on Genesis 9:2-3, Luther defines dominion after the Fall, likening it to "a tyrant who has absolute power." He also tells the reader that such dominion is proof of God's love for humankind (Martin Luther, "Lectures on Genesis, Chapters 6-14," in *Luther's Works*, edited by Jaroslav Pelikan, St. Louis: Concordia, 1960, pp. 132-134). (It is an interesting side note to remember that until the rise of colonialism, compounded by the industrial revolution, society lived rather at peace with the earth. Things began to change around the time of Rene Des Cartes, who said, "Man is the master and possessor of nature." Then the abuse of the earth began in earnest.)

Calvin (John Calvin, *Institutes of the Christian Religion*, Philadelphia: Westminster, 1960, I. xvi. 6) also insisted that "the universe was established especially for the sake of mankind." And in a more contemporary arena, even Karl Barth (d. 1968) conveyed the idea that all of the non-human creation was provided for human use according to human purposes.

In the present, even though the media has been and continues to be filled with articles and stories about all sorts of environmental concerns and disasters, Christians generally have paid minimal attention to those concerns. The fundamentalistic Christians tend to be very skeptical about the reality of an environmental crisis and view the whole topic as a "liberal" issue. There are those who view the topic generally as of no concern since the entire earth will be destroyed after the millennium anyway. Among these folks exists a subgroup that believes that the end of the world as we know it is at hand, even though the Bible is precise in reminding us that only the Father knows when the end will come (Mark 12:23). And even if that end were to come today, we would still be called to give an account of our management of the earth's resources until that event (Matt. 25:22 ff.)

Still others think that supporters of environmental concerns are guilty of false belief systems, specifically pantheism (nature and God are the same) or naturalism (all religious truths come from nature and natural causes).

For many Christians, therefore, environmental concerns are not at the forefront and often not even in the background. It is not that other science-related matters are ignored too, for the same Christians can be very vocal about evolution and genetic engineering, for example. Yet when it comes to responsibilities for preserving our shared planet and passing it on the future generations in an improved condition, most churches provide limited to no opportunities for understanding and for personal involvement.

A Christian ethic

There is a Christian ethic for the environment. The Christian ethic defines God as Creator of all things and humans as the caretakers of that creation. According to the Book of Genesis,

God told our first parents to cultivate and care for the garden. The gifts of nature can be used for the benefit of humans, but not in a manner that pollutes, wastes, or spoils the planet's ability to regenerate and give glory to God.

What sets the Christian perspective apart from the pantheistic (believing that God and nature are the same) and naturalistic (believing that all religious truth comes from natural causes and nature) perspectives is the belief that God is both transcendent and immanent. God exists above and is independent of nature. (See Psalms 19 and 24 as well as Col. 1:16-17 as examples of this perspective) Many passages also stress God's immanence in nature. "The Spirit of the Lord fills the world." Cf. Psalms 104, 139. Paul quotes approvingly two pantheistic poets (Epimenides and Aratus) in Acts 17:27b-28: "He is not far from each one of us, for in him we live and move and have our being." Luther frequently says that, "God is in the things." Luther's argument for Christ's presence in the Sacrament is from ubiquity, meaning that God and Christ fill and rule all things.

At the same time, humans were created along with other creatures but with one difference—humans were created in the image of God (Genesis 1:27). While centuries of debate continue on the precise meaning of the concept, there is general agreement that it means something like mirroring God in our moral, intellectual, and spiritual natures. Further, it includes an exclusively human ability (relative to other creatures) to make real or realize in action these natures. In summary, all creatures give glory to God by their very presence, but it is only humans who serve and worship God by an act of individual will.

This unique God-given ability carries with it the responsibility, as an act of human will, to care for rather than exploit God's creation. In practical terms at the beginning of this 21st century, this means that human dominion grants us the privilege of discovering the secrets of nature and the technologies that allow us to use nature for human benefit. This dominion, however, does not allow us to waste and pollute and spoil nature to the current or any level of abuse. The April 3, 2006 issue of *Time* magazine (www.time.com/time/magazine/article/0,9171,1176980,00.html)

defines the current situation as one in which "the climate is crashing, and global warming is to blame."

So how did we get into this mess? We have exploited virtually all created things, while believing we have the right to do so. Greed, conspicuous consumption, haste to acquire more, and the prioritizing of human demand have led to the fact that virtually every natural commodity has crossed the "tipping point" and is now on the path to depletion. If there ever was a time for the Christian ethic for the environment to become front and center in a combined effort, the time is now. This is the time to properly exercise dominion without destroying God's creation. The example of Jesus (Matt. 6:26, 10:29) telling us how much the heavenly Father cares even for sparrows, is perhaps the most basic reminder of how much God values His creation.

So, who cares?

Christians have a responsibility to the earth. Christians are not to be destroyers of the environment. God's purpose for the environment is to provide sustenance for us and pleasure for God and humans. Profit from the sustenance of the earth is not wrong but is always secondary to the protection of the environment. The Hebrew and Christian Scriptures comment throughout that God is active and involved in all spheres of the natural order.

A look at many of the Psalms will demonstrate that all the creatures, including humans, in one manner or another give testimony to the glory of God. In other parts of the Wisdom literature (Job, Proverbs, Ecclesiastes, Song of Solomon and, in the Roman Catholic tradition, also Wisdom and Ecclesiasticus), nature becomes the vehicle through which God reveals important things. In addition, this literature at least implies that God's wisdom is also revealed by observing the natural world around us. This practical heavenly wisdom is often in the form of a proverb or parable, but whatever the form its intent is to lead humans to appropriate moral behavior and away from sinful behavior. Sometimes, as in Job 38 and 39 where God first speaks from the whirlwind, we learn of God's pleasure also in non-human creatures and are reminded that they were not created just for human benefit. In all cases, God's wisdom as shared in this literature leads the reader to appreciate and respect nature and its creatures while learning from it and understanding the need to preserve it.

Again, numerous passages from St. Paul's letters (for a few examples see, Romans 8:18-25, I Corinthians 15:20-28, and Ephesians 1:10) suggest that all of creation is touched by Jesus' act of redemption and that God is concerned for all created things as we are also to be.

In addition, the places in the Bible where we are commanded to love our neighbor (Lev. 19:18, Matt. 19:19 and 22:39, Mark 12:31, Luke 10:27, Romans 13:9, Galatians 5:14, and James 2:8) also have something to say about our responsibility for the environment. This is true because so often, and maybe always, the human cost of environmental damage includes the byproduct of social injustices. How can we show love to our neighbor while being unaware or unperturbed about the environmental conditions that negatively touch their lives?

Perhaps a best summary would simply be to say that the Hebrew and Christian Scriptures strongly support respect for nature, for the creatures of nature, and for the care, protection, and preservation of everything in the natural world. These Scriptures speak boldly about our responsibility for the environment and give us much to think about as we continue to enhance a Biblical environmental ethic.

What? Me? Get involved?

Christian churches have rarely been involved in or effective at proclaiming the environment as a critical part of personal and corporate stewardship. Much of the Christian Church has spoken against materialism, genetic engineering, evolution, and abortion, as examples. But in the area of the materialism of science, demonstrated by a technological orientation toward nature, it has been largely silent. In short, the reality that we have so effectively used science to despoil the environment in the interest of profit is not generally addressed.

This may be due in part to the daily struggles we all share in trying to practice what we preach. Whether it is the environment or the many other aspects of our daily lives, confessing our personal and corporate hypocrisies, inconsistencies, and ambiguities is a consistent calling. Verbally expressing values while engaging in a lifestyle that contradicts them seems to be a part of the human condition. Acknowledging this and making conscious efforts not to justify or rationalize these contradictions is a first step in resolving them. It is a daily exercise that challenges the authenticity of our faith and the extent of our trust in the God of creation.

In addition, many fundamentalistic conservative Christians have not felt comfortable supporting environmental concerns. Often this is because, in their view, environmentalists are associated with liberals and others who support the strong role of government in this matter. Still others see the environmentalists as adherents of the New Age movement, incorporating elements of pantheism and naturalism, and have hesitated or refused to get further involved.

In spite of those concerns, however, an increasingly frightening environmental reality is beginning to surely take root within evangelical circles and, perhaps, the fundamentalist conservative Christian community. Our earth is in grave and extreme circumstances. Polar bears have no ice flows to keep them from drowning. Katrina is the prologue to our future. Mercury, arsenic, and pesticides increasingly spoil our water. Polar bears, manatees, sea otters, dolphins, sea turtles, and other wildlife are being threatened as we drill for oil in their sanctuaries and off their beaches. Yet there seems to be a growing awareness that Christian stewardship involves everything in creation. That includes how we treat what we have been given, what we give back of what we have, how we use that which we keep, and what we plan to pass on to the next generation.

Any good news?

Awareness of the need for an improved environment is growing again. Perhaps most of those seeking a better environment think that most Christians do not care about ecological issues. It is true that most local church congregations still do not provide opportunities for involvement in projects providing for ecological improvement. The witness of the Judeo-Christian Scriptures, however, reminds its followers that even though temporal history as we know it will cease, we are to still keep working for healing, including environmental healing, in the here and now.

It was an affirmation of that perspective that led the leaders of the National Association of Evangelicals (NAE) in October of 2004 to adopt and distribute to 50,000 member churches the document entitled "For the Health of the Nation: An Evangelical Call to Civic Responsibility." (www.nea.net) The document strongly endorsed the view that it was the responsibility of every Christian to take care of this planet and to appreciate the role that our government plays in safeguarding it. Because the term "environmentalism" is a negative term for many evangelicals who equate it with the Democrats and liberals, the short phrase, *creation care*, has been chosen as a better alternative. Supporters of creation care say the concept and reality is equal in importance to loving Jesus, caring for the family, and other basic theological issues.

It was hoped at that time that this public perspective would also provide the impetus for further consensus on the conflicted issue of global warming. After more than a year of trying to reach a consensus on global warming, however, the leader of the NAE, the Reverend Ted Haggard, acknowledged that such a consensus among evangelical Christians was not currently possible. (Washington Post, Feb. 2, 2006, p. A8) At issue remained the beliefs of many evangelical leaders that the reality of global warming, its causes and solutions, were still open to debate.

As might be guessed, the environmentalists within the evangelical Christian community are disappointed. Nonetheless, it can be reasonably predicted that the future is moving toward open debate among fundamentalist Christians on an issue that has, in the past, been hidden from public conversation.

How about a very brief homily?

The theologian, Karl Barth, said that all good preaching must be proclaimed with the Bible in one hand and the newspaper in the other. The great Christian musician, Johann Sebastian Bach (1865-1750), in one of his cantatas, said, *"Behold, gross darkness is in this world its evil pow'r unleashing! Why is evil to us coming? Listen well! People from the lowest to the highest, act not in righteousness before their God in dealings and find deeds lacking in love for God appealing. Thus, now instead of Light, there is darkness."* Both ideas have helped guide the comments in this book.

Only in facing up to the bad situations in which we live can we apply the Good News that the crucified Lord is risen and that fact changes our lives. What is our bad situation that we are NOT facing? What is the darkness that we are avoiding? We have heard scientists in recent decades warn us with increasing urgency that the earth's climate is going through a process of radical warming. Much, if not most, of this is due to pollution in our atmosphere. This has dire consequences for our children and generations yet unborn. But many who have raised their voices have been called "Chicken Littles," hysterically crying that the sky is falling. Sober scientists, however, on the basis of measurable evidence, are warning us that there are tell-tale signs. The warming is no longer gradual. It is escalating with alarming speed and urgency. The polar icecaps are disintegrating in both the Arctic and Antarctic. Our oceans can rise as much as 23 feet. And 70% of the world's population lives within fifty miles of seacoast. We already have experienced serious erratic changes in weather patterns.

The theologian, John Douglas Hall, wrote an important prophetic book about our failure to respond to global warming back in the 1980's. In his book, entitled, *"Lighten Our Darkness: Towards an Indigenous Theology of the Cross,"* Hall wrote that the most serious tragedy is that the United States has a *"theology of glory"* rather than a *"theology of the cross."* (Academic Renewal Press; Revised edition, May 2001) We want to talk about resurrection and optimism while refusing to face the truth of the cross. Facing that truth includes paying the cost in sacrifice to deal with the bad situation as we seek somehow to lessen its impact. The brutal truth is that we Americans cannot go on the way things are, eating up the world's energy resources and polluting our earth, water, and atmosphere without paying the piper. That's the "theology of the cross" that we must hear and heed.

President Bush recently said in his State of the Union speech that America is addicted to oil! By naming the name—addiction— can we begin on a significantly different path? If we will stare our addiction to oil in the face, this "naming the name" could possibly be the greatest initial contribution to grapple with the reality of global warming. But we must go beyond hearing the word that we are wasteful energy addicts. If any healing is to take place, there must be an about-face. Not just by us as individuals—all of our institutions and industries, and the whole American people must begin the systematized, agonizing process to make the long climb back. It must be done for ourselves, our world, and our children's children.

The reformer Martin Luther said that God upholds every rose, every kernel of grain, every blade of grass, as God permeates us and his whole world. The great liberator of India, Mahatma Gandhi, said, "Peace is not the end of the way; it is the way itself." We will not begin the long way back simply by being scared half to death about this cross we must bear. Nor will we save our world just by living spartan lives personally. We must speak and act in the public forum. We must create a climate of awareness and raise our voices, demanding that our authorities realistically lay out systematic programs to respond, calling us to disciplined realistic sacrifice—all together as a country—and beginning with our leadership and its policies.

Serious degradation of the earth, air and water has already taken place. Only if we collectively, repentantly face the facts can we slowly turn around so that this global warming does not become the apocalypse for our time. But the government must help us pay the price by leading the way. Our leaders must spell out the truth and what our regimen of sacrifice must be. Only then will we be able to rise to the challenge. Then we can say with the journalist, Eric Severeid, "I am pessimistic about tomorrow, but I am optimistic about the day after tomorrow." Not by saying it! But by living it!

Making a difference

Facing up to the realities of global warming and other environmental difficulties begins the process of bringing about change. Here are some ways in which each of us as individuals can aid in that process:

- As we live our lives and as we speak to others, we can remember that each of us is a temporary traveler on this planet and we are "trustees" with an obligation to pass it on to the next generation according to the Owners request.
- We will live with reasonable limits on ourselves, our resources, our treatment of others, our consumption, and our treatment of the environment and its fragile and delicate ecosystems.
- We will try to abide by both the laws of nature and the moral laws so that the balance of nature can continue to provide for the survival and needs of all the planet's inhabitants for all generations yet to come.
- We will never knowingly use up or destroy any resource, but will focus our actions on the needs of future generations.
- We will try to improve the environment that we received and hand it on to future generations in a more balanced and productive state.

Talking Points

- **Some fundamentalist conservatives are deeply suspicious about environmentalists.** Some believe that they should only worship God and not creation. Some believe that the end of the world and the return of Jesus are near, so worrying about ruining the environment is time wasted.
- **There is a misunderstanding of the Bible phrase that God gave "dominion" over the earth to humankind.** The proper understanding of "dominion" is that humans are

given use of the earth as a trust or as something we are borrowing. God owns the earth. Humans are not entitled to exploit it or destroy it but to use it for human benefit as God intended.

- **There is a Christian ethic for the environment.** The Christian ethic defines God as Creator of all things and humans as the caretakers of that creation. God told our first parents to cultivate and care for the garden. The gifts of nature can be used for the benefit of humans, but not in a manner that pollutes, wastes, or spoils the planet's ability to regenerate and give glory to God.

- **Christians have a responsibility to the earth.** Christians are not to be destroyers of the environment. God's purpose for the environment is to provide sustenance for us and pleasure for God and humans. Profit from the sustenance of the earth is not wrong but is always secondary to the protection of the environment.

- **Christian churches have rarely been involved in or effective at proclaiming the environment as a critical part of personal and corporate stewardship.** Much of the Christian Church has spoken against materialism, genetic engineering, evolution, and abortion, as examples. But in the area of the materialism of science, demonstrated by a technological orientation toward nature, it has been largely silent. In short, using science to despoil the environment in the interest of profit is not generally addressed.

- **Awareness of the need for an improved environment is growing again.** Perhaps most of those seeking a better environment think that most Christians do not care about ecological issues. It is true that most local church congregations do not provide opportunities for involvement in projects providing for ecological improvement. The witness of the Christian Scriptures reminds its followers that the earth will be the arena of the coming rule of God, and they are to still keep working for healing, including environmental healing, in the here and now.

8

Civics, Civility, Cooperation: We Live in Hope!

Most of us learned in high school, or before, that the study of civics included learning and interpreting the major ideas found in the U.S. Constitution and other related documents. From George Washington, who at the age of about 16 wrote 101 rules of civility, to our present understanding of the term as one showing kindness, politeness, and regard for another, civility has been a cornerstone of our society. Finally, cooperation is most simply defined as working together toward a common goal or end. This concluding chapter seeks to provide understanding, support, and encouragement for each of these three essential aspects of our living together in a common culture and working for a common good.

Our callings: religious and civic

The Gospel is calling us to a civil and informed kind of politics. The majority of the Christians in the USA are not in agreement with fundamentalistic conservative Christians like Pat Robertson and Jerry Falwell. Nor are they in agreement with the type of religious/political/ideological mixture that drives most of the current public discussion about Christianity. Nonetheless, we do need moral and ethical guidance and teaching about the basic concerns of the Judeo-Christian tradition. This includes the themes of this book: the use and misuse of wealth and power, honesty and humility, justice and mercy, sacrificing for a common good, and others. For more than a decade now, however, many sermons on a typical Sunday morning touch on subordinate issues while avoiding conversation about the priority issues in the Judeo-Christian Scriptures. The books of Moses began the conversation about honesty and truthfulness, mercy and the respect for people and property, and the need to be generous with those less fortunate. It was the Hebrew prophets who spoke eloquently and passionately about justice, mercy, and humility. They railed against injustice and bribery and human greed. When Jesus arrived on the scene, he predominantly taught about the priority of service over power, humility over pride, and the giving away of material wealth. The letters in the New Testament of the Christian Scriptures also prioritize kindness, forgiveness, generosity, self-control, peace, gentleness, meekness and goodness.

Most Christians, however, seem to be more comfortable hearing about abortion, homosexuality, and "gaming" (the gambling industry's new term to lessen the reality of its business) than about the growing disparity of wealth, the improper use of money, allotting more time to sports than service to others, and prioritizing work above everything else. Not coincidently, the subordinate issues of abortion, homosexuality, and gaming carry much more political weight than theological importance. It is that current blending of church and state that has given rise to much of the divisiveness in our culture in these days.

We are not unaware that many well-intentioned Christians still argue and believe that the United States was founded by Christians and based upon Christian principles. It is true, as we discussed earlier, that references to God and Christianity can be found. It is also the case generally that the writers of our founding documents believed in God, but not the God of Christianity. It would be much more correct to say that they were deists, believing in a "natural" religion based on human reason instead of divine revelation. The reason many of the fundamentalistic conservative Christians want our founders to be Christian is so they can use that perspective to support their political agenda. The essence of that agenda is trying to restore something they think has been lost—a nation based on Christian principles, when in reality it has not been lost because it was never there from the beginning.

Some of the other current arguments center around the contention that our founders did not have the concept of the separation of church and state in mind when they were writing the Constitution. The contention is that it was really in the 1950's and 1960's that the concept came to fore through some decisions of the Supreme Court concerning prayer in the public schools. In fact, from the writings of Roger Williams in 1644 through Thomas Jefferson in 1802 to President Ulysses Grant in 1875 to the present, the concept of separating church and state has been part and parcel of our history as a country. A far better case could be made, from the perspective of the Christian Scriptures, that the founding of our country violated the very Christian principles that the fundamentalistic conservatives want us to believe that our founders held. Given the pacifism of New Testament Christians, it is very difficult to justify an armed revolution against any ruler, including the King of England. Civil disobedience and passive resistance can be justified, but not violent revolution.

In other cultures where churches are dependent upon the government for help and support, such help and support comes at the price of religious liberty. History, indeed, seems to show that as governments try to enforce a particular brand of religion on the people, repression is the result. Conversely, the kind of church-state separation that we have provides for an open and free society where Christians, Atheists, Buddhists, Hindus, Muslims, Jews, and others live in relative religious harmony. We all can freely proclaim our beliefs and views and worship or not worship without interference by any government officials. Under our system of laws, all religions are considered equal. It was a great experiment by our founders and it is a continuing gift today.

Being right may well be wrong: but let's at least be civil

Too many Christians are not prepared to counter the claims and assertions of the fundamentalist conservative Christians. The Christian theological tradition provides compelling and understandable alternative responses to the shouted "certainties" of the religious right. It is critical at this juncture of our history for Christians to become increasingly informed about the substance of the faith they profess.

The fundamentalistic conservative Christians about whom we speak are working diligently to establish their "ideal" Christian culture. They seem to define such a culture as one where everyone believes in creationism, in eliminating the role of government in our lives as much as possible, in practicing laissez-faire capitalism, in biblical inerrancy, and essentially in only supporting the role of government in our lives to control homosexuality, abortion, and school prayer. To be more specific, they desire a society where creationism has equal billing with evolution until evolution can be totally removed from the classroom. They want to outlaw abortion, homosexuality, and welfare for the poor. They seek to eliminate liberals and humanists from the media, the schools, and the government. They want prayers and Bible reading in the public classrooms and want public funding for parochial and private schools. Finally, they want defense spending to be increased.

Another assertion of the fundamentalistic conservative Christians is that they have become victims of stereotypes promulgated by liberals and the media. A part of this "victimization" is their contention that freedom of religion applies to all other religions in America except Christianity. They suggest that current policies that are intended to protect homosexuals and other groups from discrimination, end up discriminating against conservative Christians. They also contend that while Christians can speak freely about their faith within the context of churches, they are not allowed to speak about it outside those walls. To many Christians of this variety, religious liberty means the right of others to harass Christians.

This is one reason for Christians of other persuasions to strongly affirm the increasing need for love instead of hate in our politics and our churches. These shouts of conservative Christians contending discrimination and victimization disturb other Christians and concerned citizens who strongly disagree. At root, these folks seek to intrude into our most dearly held religious experiences and into our health decisions and family life. They threaten our personal liberties by using Jesus Christ inappropriately to support their own political agenda and to work toward a merging of church and state.

To help counter the claims and assertions of the fundamentalistic conservative Christians, it is important to challenge and confront them and their revisions and distortions of history and the Judeo-Christian Scriptures. It is important for the rest of us to assert the lack of their ethics in providing biased guides for voting and distributing them in churches, in surreptitiously placing candidates who conceal their extreme religious views up for election as school board members and other offices, and in intimidating and browbeating public officials. Perhaps they have not read the prophet Isaiah's reminder that "in quietness and confidence shall be our strength" (Isaiah 30:15). It is also important that we communicate our values and views "in quietness and confidence" to our leaders, that we vote for leaders who stand with courage for our historic religious liberty, and that we morally and financially support those who seek to remind Americans of this exceptional liberty.

Christians as "little Christs"

While Christians have generally pondered the words and works of Jesus and how they reflect an ideological perspective, they have often differed on what that perspective is. In fact, it is an ideological mixture of people who show themselves to be the feet and hands of Jesus. As individuals, these are often the people who work in various types of shelters, serve in food kitchens and volunteer in food pantries, and promote international peace and harmony. Conservatives and liberals alike can be very good at individual charity. It is the broad dimensions of social justice and the biblical mandate for such justice that conservative fundamentalists often don't understand. It is time for liberal Christians to reassert the importance of a faith that shows itself in good works.

It is, of course, easy to say that and difficult to live it. Many Americans, and perhaps most people, find the poor and disenfranchised and powerless and marginal and ill to be depressing or scary or dangerous or different or worthy of disdain. But according to the Judeo-Christian Scriptures, God is compassionate toward these humans. If God compassionately values people at the margins of society, and God is to be our model, then the message is very simple. God calls each of us to affirm and support them. That is not a message that is hard to understand but it is hard to accomplish.

It is compelling that the message of compassionately serving those in need is consistent throughout the Judeo-Christian Scriptures. This message is found in the Torah, the Psalms and Prophets, the Gospels, and in the Epistles. In all cases, there is no allowance for excuses not to be of service and no excuses for lack of help are offered. God just wants us to give aid and assistance to people in any need, without qualification. This includes people specifically identified in previous chapters. God even specifies those to whom we are to give relief: the stranger, the traveler, the alien, people who are not like us, people who cannot repay us, people of a different race or religion, the poor and needy.

A few more things can still be said. While moderation is generally good, being immoderate is the Biblical expectation when it comes to offering assistance to those in need. Also, adding to the hurt and misery of the poor is not the norm to which we are called. This includes behaviors like taking from the needy to make the rich richer, exploiting workers, oppressing the immigrants, or simply ignoring the needs of the poor and others. As an aside, the Old Testament city of Sodom was not destroyed for sexual morality as we mentioned earlier, but for "arrogance, abundant food, and careless ease" and "it did not help the poor and needy." Ouch!

Finally, we are called to become defenders and advocates for the needy—to speak for them and defend them and keep their needs before the people with whom we associate. While Jesus was neither a Republican nor a Democrat, he was a revolutionary in the sense that he lived as one among the poor and put himself in their place. Some of his followers today act in accordance with how they apparently think Jesus should have acted—as a powerful and prestigious and rich leader, with huge and extravagant buildings and an audience of millions and glitter and noise and material success. But Jesus came and lived and ministered as a poor person. He took the issue of need very personally. A culture or church whose supreme deity is wealth and money, while ignoring the needy, is marching 180 degrees opposite of the path Jesus took. It is the path that Jesus took that previous chapters have attempted to identify in terms of a variety of people in need.

More about we—a spirit of cooperation

Other people and other faiths share important values with Christians. A primary question common to Christians is "who is my neighbor?" The answer is "anyone in need." It is important for Christians to work in the political and secular sphere with anyone who shares that desire to serve a "neighbor" in need, Christian or not. One does not have to be a Christian to share Christian values. Christians do not limit living their faith in acts of love and service only with other Christians.

These assertions are based on Jesus' response to the religious leaders of his day when they asked him to identify the greatest of God's commandments. He quoted Deuteronomy 6:5 (You shall love the Lord your God with all your heart, with all your soul, and with all your strength.) as the greatest commandment, but quickly followed that by adding "You shall love your neighbor as yourself" (Matthew 22:39, cf. Leviticus 19:18). When a lawyer asked Jesus who our neighbor is (Luke 10:29), he told the story of the Good Samaritan to demonstrate the point that anyone and everyone who touches our life with any need should be responded to with love as we seek to meet that need. The previous chapters have attempted to identify some of those needs and a Christ-like response to them.

It is easy to love people we like and are familiar with, but according to Judeo-Christian beliefs, the image of God was placed into every human at creation. It is still a part of every human, whether an outcast or enemy or alien or terrorist or church elder. As such, we are called to treat every human with self-giving love and compassion because of the image of God within that person. Part of the mischief of the past for those of the Judeo-Christian perspective, which spills over into the present, is the fact that the rabbinical practice during Jesus' time defined enemies in a manner that excluded them from being neighbors. Not loving those that were hated led to all sorts of harmful, unkind, and disrespectful behaviors, not unlike today. Jesus, however, said "You have heard that it was said, 'Love your neighbor and hate your enemy.' But I tell you: Love your enemies and pray for those who persecute you. (Matthew 5:43)" It is a difficult saying, but expressing love toward even our enemies is one of the identifiers of followers of Jesus.

But it begins with me

We are not happy for the Christian faith to be caricatured by James Dobson, Jerry Falwell, George W. Bush, and others of similar perspective. These are people who exemplify the concern expressed by Pascal that "men never do evil so fully and so happily as when they do it for conscience's sake." On the other hand, it was Einstein, among others, who reminded us that "the world is a dangerous place. Not because of the people who are evil, but because of the people who won't do anything about it." And so we begin again to do something about it.

It is good to remember that fundamentalists have apparently always been with us. As mentioned earlier, however, there has been a fairly recent resurgence in fundamentalism throughout the world, beginning between thirty and forty years ago. Nonetheless, from the Catholic fundamentalist crusades against the Moors to the Protestant fundamentalist terrorism against the Irish Catholics; from the Sikh fundamentalist who killed Indira Gandhi to the Jewish fundamentalist who killed Yitzhak Rabin; from the Muslim fundamentalists that took over Iran to the Christian Protestant fundamentalists that are abusing our nation, none of them have lived or now live according to the realities of the faiths they pretend to represent. No. Fundamentalists of any stripe or shade are really, in their practices, zealots. Zealots have a fervent and even militant belief in the rightness of their positions. They believe that everyone else must be made to believe the same "truths" that they hold dear.

So what has happened is that even though all of the religions mentioned above are peace-loving in their belief systems, the fundamentalists, who can be judgmental, mean, angry, abrasive, and even frightening, have led followers of all these faiths to fear even some in their own faith. Christians are afraid of some Christians, Muslims are afraid of some Muslims, Jews are afraid of some Jews, and the like. This has become a reality also in our time because zealots do not easily respond to reason, logic, or good argumentation. To disagree with one belief of theirs is to challenge all their beliefs, which threatens their world view in its entirety. If you don't agree with them, you are "lost" or "blinded by Satan" or "possessed by Satan" or a "tool of Satan."

But this is not the time to take these attacks personally, or to live in the kind of fear that fundamentalists try to use to bring about the conformity they desire. In fact, it is best not to take them seriously, but to empathize with them for the rigid straitjacketed thinking in which they are trapped. This is a time to offer the opportunity for healing that love, kindness, and care can offer.

Again, these are easy words to say but difficult words to implement. It requires working at being friends with those in strong disagreement with us. It requires treating fundamentalists with respect and care even if they condemn and revile us. It requires showing them through our actions that they are valued as human beings, in the image of God, even if they do not reciprocate. Until we can authentically value them for who they are, God's children, we cannot expect them to be open to another avenue of "truth."

We, of course, also need to remember that change on such value-laden issues as those covered in this book comes slowly. It has not been too many decades ago, for example, that the same verses from the Judeo-Christian Scriptures that were used to devalue African-Americans, support slavery, and subjugate women, sound much too much like the verses that are used today to devalue homosexuals and other groups. It was leaders of the church also then, confidently using Bible verses, who insisted that it was a part of God's plan for those "especially sinful and morally inferior" folks to be treated in a manner that today we define as sinful.

The words of the Bible, of course, have remained the same. The Church and society have, however, changed. Because they have changed, we have changed and are capable of continuing change in the way in which we read and understand the Bible. Especially in this day and time we are discerning anew that seeking understanding by looking for "proof" texts in the Bible without trying to understand those texts through the lens of Jesus' words and work is like missing the forest because of the trees. May the church's history open our eyes to the grace-filled future that awaits us.

Some final thoughts

When it comes to the practice of religion in our country, there can be positive or negative circles of activity. Because of the wisdom of our founders who "preached" the concept of religious tolerance, religious liberty became one of our freedoms. With religious liberty came the gift of religious diversity which always leads back to the beginning of the circle—religious tolerance. In that way, the circle of religion in America has predominantly remained complete and positive. Conversely, if the circle is reversed in its movement, religious intolerance often can limit religious liberty. As religious liberty is limited, religious diversity also tends to be limited. The final result historically would be a consistently renewing religious intolerance.

It is our fear that we are moving toward that reality in our culture. When "religious" organizations like Focus on the Family, the Moral Majority Coalition, or the Liberty Alliance, as examples, try to influence or control political processes through organized partisan behaviors, they taint any appearance of religious impartiality on the part of those they may have helped elect. If, in the process, any part of the government appears to show religious favoritism, religious differences are accentuated, religious tolerance is reduced, and religious groups are emboldened in their attempts to increase control of the political processes.

In short, as "religious" organizations move into an open political partisanship in the electoral processes, they lose their proper focus. It is proper for such organizations to appropriately share and defend their religious beliefs about all aspects of our daily lives, but not within the context of a partisan political perspective. It is improper for them to abdicate their moral authority by seeking to use the electoral processes to inflict their partisan beliefs on others. Concurrently, should they be successful, and should those who are elected begin to feel that they owe their election to a particular religious group or organization, everyone's religious liberty is in the process of being threatened.

Finally, neither the religious left nor the religious right has a monopoly on theological truth. What either perspective wants to believe as Christians is their business. But none of us have the right, through the coercion of power, to foist these beliefs on civil society. We certainly operate out of our religious beliefs in the public arena, but within that arena our main focus should be on upholding the vision of our founders and our founding documents, which were informed by reason, justice, and what was perceived to be natural law, as for example, "we hold these truths to be self-evident." Our role should be to restore civil debate, and the way to do that is through a re-emphasis on civics, civility, and cooperation.

We close, then, with this reminder from Wendell Phillips (1811-1884): "Eternal vigilance is the price of liberty—power is ever stealing from the many to the few. The hand entrusted with power becomes . . . the enemy of the people. Only by continual oversight can the democrat in office be prevented from hardening into a despot: only by unintermitted agitation can people be kept sufficiently awake to principle not to let liberty be smothered in material prosperity." (Boston, Massachusetts, January 28, 1852)

Making a difference

Civics, civility, and cooperation. Here are some ways we can demonstrate our understanding of and appreciation for these concepts:

- In all ways, act in love and seek to serve others.
- Work to aid others in achieving their potential by being sensitive to the whole person—emotional, physical, spiritual, and intellectual.
- Anger usually communicates a need that is not met and violence is often the language of the unheard. Listen to the angry as a means of meeting a need and ameliorating violence.
- Remember that any label that does not carry the connotation of "we" is a label that separates people from the rest of society.
- None of us is totally independent. We all depend on others for many things and others need to also depend on us for unmet needs.
- Avoid any behaviors that demean, devalue, or degrade another human. Whether such behaviors are unintended or deliberate, they dehumanize another and produce feelings of loneliness, frustration, and separation.
- Our behavior tends to be contagious. Being a good role model can significantly influence others.
- Take the risk of openness toward those to whom you have been closed. Without risk, there can be no growth and limited dignity. With risk, the potential for change is unlimited.

Talking Points

- **The Gospel is calling us to a civil and informed kind of politics.** The majority of the Christians in the USA are not in agreement with fundamentalist conservative Christians like Pat Robertson and Jerry Falwell. Nor are they in agreement with the type of religious/political ideological mixture that drives most of the current public discussion about Christianity. Most continue to prefer a major building block of our democracy, the separation of church and state.

- **Too many Christians are not prepared to counter the claims and assertions of the fundamentalist conservative Christians.** The Christian theological tradition provides compelling and understandable alternative responses to the shouted "certainties" of the religious right. It is critical at this juncture of our history for Christians to become increasingly informed about the substance of the faith they profess.

- **Christians generally have not reflected on the words and works of Jesus and how they reflect an ideological perspective.** It is an ideological mixture of people who show themselves to be the feet and hands of Jesus. As individuals, these are primarily the people who work in various types of shelters, serve in food kitchens and volunteer in food pantries, and promote international peace and harmony. Conservatives and liberals alike can be very good at individual charity. It is the broad dimensions of social justice and the biblical mandate for such justice that conservative fundamentalists don't understand. It is time for liberal Christians to reassert the importance of a faith that shows itself in good works.

- **Other people and other faiths share important Christian values.** A primary question common to Christians is "who is my neighbor?" The answer is "anyone in need." It is important for Christians to work in the political and secular sphere with anyone who shares that desire to serve a "neighbor" in need, Christian or not. One does not have to be a Christian to share Christian values. Christians do not limit living their faith in acts of love and service only with other Christians.

- **It begins with me.** We are not happy for the Christian faith to be caricatured by James Dobson and George W. Bush. These are people who exemplify the concern expressed by Pascal that "men never do evil so fully and so happily as when they do it for conscience's sake." On the other hand, it was Einstein, among others, who reminded us that "the world is a dangerous place. Not because of the people who are evil, but because of the people who won't do anything about it." And so we begin again to do something about it.

ACKNOWLEDGEMENTS

I t was out of the care and concern for the election results in 2000 and 2004 that the seeds of this book were planted. It was in the hope for political and religious change that we committed ourselves to a very short timetable to research and write this volume. None of it, however, would have been possible without the help of many people.

First, we wish to thank our spouses and children who encouraged us, forgave us, critiqued us, and affirmed us. Our spouses, Elizabeth A. Bruch and Doris E. Strieter, are both very busy professionals themselves who nonetheless always shared the time even under stressful circumstances to provide incisive editorial advice.

Second, we would offer special thanks to Doris Strieter for her work especially on the "Haves and Have-Nots" chapter as well as on portions of other chapters. In addition, her editing and organizational skills have helped to make this readable to a much larger group of people. While we remain trapped in a skill set that works best within the confines of academia and professional ministry, Doris is a "real people" person with an eye for "real people" conversation.

Third, we are very grateful for the editing skills of Elizabeth M. Bruch who took valuable time from her law school teaching to acquiesce to our cries for help. Her own publishing experience and professional writing have surely helped her to smooth many of the rough edges of the manuscript.

Finally, Tricia Christiansen and her very able staff (*www.christiansencreative.com*) have generously given of their time and skill to design the book cover, help in the marketing, and always encourage us in the writing of the book.

Of course, even while we thank them all, we do assure you that any shortcomings, errors, omissions, or oversights are totally our responsibility.

Daniel C. Bruch is a retired pastor, professor, and social activist. He has earned six degrees (including the D.Min., Ph.D., and Sc.D.); served as a college, university, and seminary professor; been a parish pastor and university chaplain; volunteered as a certified emergency room, police, and prison chaplain; and is a certified mediator and arbitrator. He is and has been involved in civil and human rights, women's rights, gay rights, just war, and economic justice. He became a liberal by conviction, not by birth. He has taught in Romania, Serbia, Hungary, and Indonesia. Dr. Bruch is a founder and President of Live Liberal (www.liveliberal.org). He resides in Hudson, WI

Thomas W. Strieter is a retired Lutheran minister and professor with an STM and a PhD in Theology. His years in the ministry have been divided between the parish and academia. He has served as a professor of theology in both Protestant and Catholic colleges and universities, teaching courses in biblical studies, history of Christian thought, and ethics. He is a certified counselor in mediation and conflict resolution; an activist in civil rights, peace movements, and other human rights and social justice issues; and has served as an elected public official in a multi-racial Chicago suburb. He has twice served in Bali as a teacher and pastor, and has written theological journal articles and several books on Luther and Reformation studies. He lives in Chicago, Illinois.